BIBLE TALES

THE PUBLICATION OF THIS
VOLUME WAS MADE POSSIBLE
BY THE ESTABLISHMENT OF A
FUND FOR THE PUBLICATION
OF JEWISH RELIGIOUS SCHOOL
LITERATURE
BY
THE NATIONAL FEDERATION
OF TEMPLE SISTERHOODS

BIBLE TALES

For Very Young Children

BY LENORE COHEN

Union of American Hebrew Congregations

CINCINNATI, 1934

Tenth Printing

Copyright, 1934
BY
The Union of American Hebrew Congregations
PRINTED IN THE UNITED STATES OF AMERICA

IN LOVING MEMORY OF

MY PARENTS

MAX COHEN

AND

FRIEDA LASER COHEN

Editor's Introduction

WHAT!" the reader will say, "another book of Bible stories? Haven't we enough books in which Bible stories are told and retold?"

And yet, we found it necessary to prepare a new text of Bible stories for little children. Many a writer of juvenile stories believes that an abbreviated story is a good story for children. As a matter of fact, the opposite is the case. While the adult can read and enjoy a narrative or an exposition that is, on the whole, condensed and concise, children require a story that goes into detail, that is vivid and concrete.

Then the problem of selecting Bible stories for the early grades is an especially difficult one. Not all the stories of the Bible are suited to the needs of little children, nor should all those chosen be told in their entirety. In some instances certain details should be omitted; in others they should be inserted.

Another problem is that of emphasis. A Bible story should be told in such a way that the underlying idea is inherent in the telling of it without attaching the main thought at the end, as the proverbial "moral to the tale." The present book of Bible stories is an attempt to solve all the above problems. Whether or not those who use this text will agree with us in every respect, the author has attempted to meet the needs of little children, bearing in mind both the values of the Bible and what recent educational theory has to teach us in this connection.

The stories were furthermore prepared with the idea of their

being told by the mother in the home or by the teacher in the class-
room to children so young that they have not yet learned to read.
Hence the conversational tone and the possibilities for dramatiza-
tion inherent in these stories. With this in mind, we have secured
the services of Miss Penina Kishore, who, we believe, has succeeded
in illustrating the stories, so charmingly told by Miss Cohen, with
drawings equally charming and appropriate.

We trust that mothers and teachers will find our book helpful
in developing in our little children a love for our great book, the
Bible.

EMANUEL GAMORAN

Table of Contents

BIBLE TALES

Abraham Breaks the Idols

OUR first story is not found in the Bible, but it is a famous story that Jewish people have been telling to their children for thousands of years. It helps us to understand the life of our first hero, Abraham.

When Abraham was a little boy, he lived in the land of Ur. This country of Ur was a very wicked country. All the people worshiped idols. Idols were large dolls made of wood or stone. The people bowed before these idols because they thought that the idols had made the world. But Abraham's father had made the idols. He kept them all together in a room by themselves. There were big idols, little idols, and tiny little idols. Abraham liked to go into this room and play with the idols.

He would say, "Big idol, you are the father; and medium-sized idol, you are the mother; and tiny idols, you are the children." In this way he had much fun playing games with the idols.

Now Abraham's father did not know of the queer game his little boy liked to play. One day he had to go away and he said, "Abraham, take good care of the idols while I am gone."

"Yes, father," answered Abraham.

No sooner had his father gone than Abraham began to play his favorite game. The children idols became naughty and the father idol had to punish them. Now, of course, an idol can't punish anyone; so Abraham put a big stick in the father idol's hand and he pretended that he was punishing the children. Suddenly, Abraham heard a crash! Turning around, he saw that he had broken two of the most beautiful idols in the room by knocking them off the table with the end of his stick.

Abraham was greatly frightened. He heard his father's steps coming back, tap, tap, tap, along the stones. He did not know what to do. Suddenly he had an idea. He put the stick back in the father idol's hand.

Abraham's father came into the house. He saw

"Wicked boy, see what you have done."

3

his beautiful idols broken! He cried, "Wicked boy, see what you have done!"

Abraham answered, "But, father, I did not break them. See the stick in the father idol's hand? He punished the children idols because they were wicked."

"An idol cannot punish anyone," said his father.

"Then why do you bow down to him?" asked Abraham.

Abraham's father looked at the wooden idol with its flat, smiling face. He looked at the clumsy wooden hands which could not move. He said, "There is wisdom in what you say, my boy. There must be some great idol who rules the world."

"There is no idol, but a great God, whom we cannot see. I have heard His voice and in my dreams He has told me of a land more beautiful than this, where we shall live some day," said Abraham.

"You must wait until you are a man," answered his father. "Then you will travel to the far-away land."

"We are the shepherds who tend the sheep,
Under the stars we eat and sleep;
Ever we wander, ever we roam,
The plain and the desert is our home."

ABRAHAM stood in front of his tent. He was a tall man, sunburned and strong. All these hundreds of sheep were his. All the shepherds who were watering the sheep were his servants.

Sarah, his wife, came out of the tent and stood beside him.

"What are you thinking about, Abraham?" she asked.

"I am thinking of a dream I had last night," he replied. "I seemed to stand alone in a field. Suddenly I heard the voice of God saying, 'Abraham, leave your father's house. Go to the west. There is a land of green pastures and silver streams. I will bless you, Abraham. You will be the father of a great nation.' "

"Is there really such a land?" asked Sarah.

"Yes," answered Abraham. "Look! What do you see, far in the distance?"

"Mountain tops, which look like huge, black points against the setting sun."

"There is the land I dreamed about. Tomorrow we shall rise with the dawn and start to travel there."

Abraham blew a shrill whistle. All the shepherds came running. At their head came Lot, Abraham's nephew.

"Herd all the sheep and cattle together. Pack up the tents and all our household goods. We leave this place at dawn."

"Where are we going, Abraham?" asked Lot.

"To the mountains. To a new country! A country where I can worship the one Almighty God in peace."

What a hustle and bustle there was. At dawn everything was ready. Abraham, tall and brave, rode at the head of his household on a camel. Sarah rode beside him, while the shepherds and their wives and children followed behind. They moved slowly, for the sheep and goats had to be kept together. In this manner they traveled for many days.

At last they came to the mountains. How green and inviting they seemed!

"Let us stop here," said Abraham.

The animals were unloaded; the tents were set up; fires were built. Abraham climbed to the top of the mountain so that he could be alone. There he built an altar and prayed to God.

The next day Abraham took Lot to the top of the mountain. They could see the country around them. The cattle were spread over the mountain like a blanket. How greedily they nibbled the slender tufts of grass! The little calves tried to edge in and get a bite of the sweet grass, too, but the cows crowded them out. It seemed strange that such large herds of cattle should be huddled together on one mountain, when miles of fertile pasture stretched out around them. To make it worse, Lot's shepherds were quarreling with Abraham's shepherds.

"Get your cattle out of the way!" cried Lot's shepherds angrily. "Can't you leave some grass for us?"

"This isn't the only place where grass grows. Isn't there plenty of other pasture land?" cried Abraham's shepherds.

"Take your cattle away or we will drive them off!" Lot's shepherds began to fight.

"Peace! Peace! This is no time for quarrels." It was Abraham speaking. He had come down from the mountain top at the sound of the angry voices.

The shepherds stopped their quarreling at the sound of Abraham's gentle but firm tone of voice.

"Look at the beautiful country about us," said Abraham. "There is too much land to quarrel over pastures. Let us each go a different way. Lot, look about you. Which way do you choose? Right or left?"

Lot looked out over the plain. There was the beautiful river Jordan flowing through the middle of the land. There were two cities, Sodom and Gomorrah, which looked like gardens. Lot said, "I will choose the plain of the river Jordan."

So Lot gathered all that belonged to him and traveled east.

When Lot had gone, Abraham heard the voice of God saying, "Look, Abraham, look to the east; look to the west; look to the north; look to the south. All the land that you see, I give to you and your children forever. Rise and walk through the land. All of it belongs to you."

Abraham walked all over the land, as God had told him to do. Under some large oak trees, in a place called Mamre, he made his home and built an altar to God.

Abraham Saves Lot

ONE night Abraham was awakened by the barking of the watchdogs outside his tent. As he stepped outside to see what was happening, a man fell on the ground at his feet. The man was breathing hard. His clothing was torn, and his body was covered with scratches and bruises.

"Who are you?" cried Abraham.

"I—come—from Lot. He has been taken captive."

"From Lot, my nephew?" Abraham thought of the day when Lot had chosen to settle near the cities of Sodom and Gomorrah. Now those cities were being attacked. The inhabitants were being carried off as slaves. All their household goods were stolen.

"I, alone, escaped," the man went on. "The enemy has captured the five kingdoms around you. They are not far from here now."

"Who are you?"

11

When Abraham heard this terrible news, he said, "We must march against the enemy at once. Rouse the men in the camp. See that they are well armed."

Within a very few hours Abraham was on his way. He had three hundred men, all brave and strong.

They came upon the enemy at night. Happy over their victory, the soldiers were eating and drinking in celebration. Imagine their surprise when Abraham charged in upon them with his well-trained men. Within a very short time, Abraham had driven them far into the wilderness. All the stolen goods was left behind, and with cries of joy, the people who were with Abraham brought the goods back to their owners.

But Abraham was happy when he found Lot and his family unharmed. He took nothing for himself. The King of Sodom asked him why he would not take anything.

Abraham answered, "I came here to rescue my nephew, Lot, and his family. Now that I have found him I ask nothing more. All of you have suffered at the hands of the enemy. Divide the spoils among you."

Abraham then started back home. Wherever he went people came out to greet him. They all honored and loved him for the great kindness of his heart.

The King of Salem, who was a priest of God, brought Abraham bread and wine, and blessed him, saying, "Blessed be Abraham of God most high, maker of heaven and earth."

Abraham Is Kind to Strangers

THE sun was in the middle of the sky. It was noon. In Palestine the noonday sun is very hot. The air is dry and there is little wind. Three men were walking across the plain. They moved slowly, for the sun was so hot. Not a stream was to be seen. There was not a single tree under which they might rest.

"It is very hot," said the first. "I wish I might have some place to rest."

"I am so thirsty," said the second, "I wish I might have a drink of water."

"I am so hungry," said the third, "I wish I could have something to eat."

"Look!" cried the first. "At the foot of the hill are some trees."

"There is a tent and a man is sitting in front of it!" cried the second.

"Look!" cried the first.

15

"I wonder if he will let us eat there," cried the third.

The three men began to walk toward the tent. When they were close to the trees, a man ran out to meet them. The man was Abraham.

"Come under my trees and rest yourselves," he said. "I will bring water so that you can wash your feet. I will bring bread so that you can eat."

The men sat down under the trees and said, "Thank you. We will do as you have said."

Abraham went into his tent. He said to Sarah, his wife, "Be quick, take some meal and make some good cakes of it."

Sarah began to make the cakes. Abraham went out to the hillside where his herd of cattle was feeding. He said to the shepherd, "Take one of our finest calves; prepare it and cook it, for we have visitors with us today."

Soon the meal was ready. Abraham brought the cakes and meat to the men. They sat under the trees and ate, and drank the cool water, for they were very hungry and thirsty. When they had finished, they said, "Where is Sarah, your wife?"

"She is inside the tent," Abraham answered.

Then the men said, "We will come back again, for you have been very kind to us. When we come back, Sarah will have a son."

Sarah was standing inside the tent door. When she heard that she would have a son, she was very happy. For Sarah wanted a son more than anything else in the world.

Ishmael Is Saved

THERE was great joy in Abraham's tent. Sarah had a son. She said:

"God filled my heart with joy,
He gave to me a baby boy."

Sarah and Abraham named the boy Isaac. Isaac grew very quickly. He was a large, strong boy. Now Abraham had another wife, whose name was Hagar. Hagar was an Egyptian woman and she was also Sarah's servant. Hagar had a son, too. His name was Ishmael. Ishmael was a bad boy. He was always getting into mischief. He tormented the goats and the sheep, and he shouted at the top of his voice. He was older and larger than Isaac. He was always hurting Isaac and making him unhappy. Sarah did not like to see Ishmael hurting her boy and many times she said to Hagar, "Hagar, please tell Ishmael not to hurt Isaac. He is so much stronger and older than Isaac. He should take care of him, instead of hurting him."

Hagar did not tell Ishmael that he was doing wrong. Things became worse every day. At last Sarah said to Abraham, "You must send Hagar away. I have tried to be kind to her and to her son, but they do not listen. I cannot be made unhappy any longer."

Abraham loved Sarah very much. Yet he felt sorry for the poor servant woman, Hagar, and her boy, who was his son. He went off to a place where he could be alone. He prayed to God, saying, "Oh, God, tell me what I should do."

God said to Abraham, "Do not be sad, Abraham. Listen to what Sarah has told you. It is better that Hagar and her son should leave your house. I will watch over them and take care of them."

The next morning Abraham called Hagar and her son to him.

"Here is plenty of food and water, Hagar. You must go away from here. Do not be afraid, for God will take care of you."

"Rest under this tree."

20

Hagar put the food and water on her shoulder. She took Ishmael by the hand. Together they walked into the great forest beyond. They wandered for several days. All the food and water were gone. Ishmael was tired and thirsty; night was coming on.

"I am so tired, Mother," he said, "can't you give me some water to drink?"

Hagar did not answer. There was not a drop of water anywhere. She could hardly look at the tired, thirsty boy. At last she said, "Rest under this tree."

Hagar walked away from the boy. She began to cry loudly, "Oh, God, please save my boy!"

Then Hagar heard a voice. "Do not be afraid, Hagar," it said. "Take your boy by the hand and keep him close to you. I will take care of you."

Hagar could not see anyone. She looked all around and there, right before her, was a large fountain of water. Hagar was so happy that she cried with joy. She filled the bottle with water and gave Ishmael a drink.

From that day on, Hagar never left Ishmael. God watched over them both. Ishmael always lived in the forest and grew up to be a great hunter.

In Place of Isaac

~⊘~

DAWN had just come up over the hills. The moon was still peeping from behind the clouds, and the birds were chirping a very sleepy song. In the plain stood Abraham's blue and white tent.

"Get up, Isaac," Abraham called. "Get up, Isaac, another day is here."

"Why must I get up so early?" asked the boy. "The moon is still out and even the sheep are half asleep. Can't I sleep a little longer?"

"We are going on a journey. See, the boys are here with the donkeys. We are all ready to start."

Isaac rubbed his eyes and dressed himself slowly. Abraham watched the boy tenderly. In his old age, God had given him this beautiful boy. How tall and strong he was! How young and happy he seemed! Last night Abraham had heard a voice calling. It was the voice of God, who said, "Abraham!"

"Here I am," answered Abraham.

"Take your only son, Isaac," God said, "and go into the land of Moriah. There I will show you a high mountain, where you must make a sacrifice of your son, Isaac."

Then all was silent. Abraham could not sleep the rest of the night. He waited for dawn. With the first signs of morning, he awakened two servant boys. He said, "Load the donkeys with plenty of food and wood, for we are going on a long journey."

"I am ready now," Isaac called cheerfully. "Where are we going, Father?"

"To the land of Moriah," answered Abraham sadly. If he talked to the boy, he might not be able to go on. So, silently, he led the way and helped the boy get up on the donkey.

They traveled for three days. At last they came to Mount Moriah. It stood high above the other peaks. The top of it seemed lost in clouds.

"This is the mountain," said Abraham. "Both of you boys stay here with the donkeys. Isaac and I will climb up the mountain. We will make a sacrifice and come back to you.

23

"*. . . How can we make a sacrifice without a lamb?*"

"Isaac, you take the wood. I will take the fire."

Isaac took the wood from the donkeys' backs. He followed his father, who had begun to climb the mountain.

"Father," Isaac called.

"Yes?"

"We have wood and fire, but how can we make a sacrifice without a lamb?"

"God will give us a lamb for a sacrifice," answered Abraham.

They climbed higher and higher. Soon they came to a place where the ground was flat.

"We will make our sacrifice here," said Abraham. He built an altar and piled it high with wood. Then he took his son Isaac and laid him on the altar. His hand trembled; he could see nothing, for his eyes were blinded by tears. Suddenly the voice of God called from Heaven, "Abraham, Abraham!"

"Here I am," answered Abraham.

"Do not lay your hand on your son! Do not hurt him! Now I know how much you love God. You have not even kept your son from me; but I do not want child sacrifice."

25

Abraham fell to the ground and wept. Isaac was dearer to him than anything in the world. Suddenly he heard a noise. He looked around to see what it could be. There was a young ram caught by the horns in some thick bushes.

Abraham caught the ram. He placed it on the altar as a sacrifice instead of Isaac. Then he kissed his son and said, "I shall call this place 'In the mount where the Lord is seen.'"

Soon he heard the voice of God again. "Since you were willing to give me your only son, I will bless you and all who come after you. For you have listened to my voice."

Abraham was so happy; he kissed Isaac again and again.

Then Abraham and Isaac climbed down the mountain. They found the boys waiting for them. Together they returned home.

Rebekah Is Chosen

ABRAHAM had grown to be a very old man. One day he called his servant Eliezer to him and said, "I am very old, Eliezer, and my days are numbered. There is one thing I want you to promise me faithfully."

"What is it?" asked Eliezer.

"Give me your hand," said Abraham solemnly.

Eliezer placed his hand in the hand of his master.

"Promise me that you will find a wife among my own people for my son Isaac. Yet beware of one thing! Do not allow my son to go back into that country."

"Suppose the woman will not follow me back into this new and unsettled country?" asked Eliezer.

"If the woman refuses to follow you, you are free from your promise."

"I promise faithfully," said Eliezer.

The next day he set forth on his journey. He took ten camels with him. After a few days, he came to a city.

A beautiful fountain stood in the center of the city. The water was very clear and cool. All the people of the city came to this fountain for their drinking water. Eliezer saw some young girls coming to the fountain. They held water jugs on their shoulders. As they dipped the jugs into the fountain, they sang this song:

"Fountain silver, fountain bright,
Cool by day, cool by night;
Fountain springing from the ground,
Clearest fountain to be found."

There was one girl who was more beautiful than all the rest. She had long black hair and brown eyes. Her name was Rebekah.

Suddenly the girls saw Eliezer standing there. They looked at the ten camels with him. He looked as though he had come from a long journey, for his clothes were very dusty.

Eliezer stepped up to one of the girls and said:

"Let down your pitcher, daughter fair,
That I may drink some water there."

The girl did not answer him. She was afraid of his
dirty clothes. She started to run away. Rebekah
could see that Eliezer was a good man, so she dipped
her pitcher into the fountain, saying:

"My Lord, I pray you, water drink,
Come closer to the fountain's brink;
Your camels must be thirsty, too,
I'll give them water when you're through."

Eliezer drank the water. He watched Rebekah as
she ran back and forth, drawing water for the camels.
He said, "You are very kind to me. Whose daughter
are you?"

"I am the daughter of Bethuel," said Rebekah.

When Eliezer heard the name Bethuel, he said to
himself, "She is the girl I am looking for. God is
with me." Then he knelt on the ground and said to
Rebekah, "Take this ring and bracelet."

Rebekah had never seen such beautiful gifts before. She did not dare to take them from him.

"My lord, I pray you drink."

Eliezer said, "Do not be afraid. Take these gifts for your kindness to me."

Rebekah put the ring and bracelet on her hands.

"I am a stranger in this city," said Eliezer. "Could your father make room for me at his house tonight?"

"We have plenty of room. I am sure we could give you shelter tonight," said Rebekah. "I will go home and tell my mother about you first."

So Rebekah ran home. There she told her mother about the man at the fountain.

Rebekah had a brother whose name was Laban. When he heard Rebekah's story, he said, "I will go down to the fountain and bring the man and his camels home."

Laban brought Eliezer home. He gave shelter to the camels. Then he took Eliezer into the house and gave him water to wash himself. He also gave him something to eat. But Eliezer said, "I will not eat until I have told you who I am."

"Tell us," said Laban.

"I am your uncle Abraham's servant. Abraham is a very rich man. He has large herds of goats and sheep. He has many servants. He also has much gold and silver."

"Why has Abraham sent you here?" asked Laban.

"He sent me here to find a wife for his son Isaac. Abraham wants Isaac to marry a girl from among his own people. As I stood by the fountain, I was very thirsty. Rebekah was kind to me. She gave water to me and my camels. When I asked her name, I found she was Isaac's cousin."

Laban answered, "Rebekah is here. If she wishes to go with you, she will be Isaac's wife."

When Abraham's servant heard these words, he bowed very low. "Here are gifts from my master." He gave Rebekah and her family much gold and silver.

Very early the next morning Eliezer began to get ready to go away.

Rebekah's mother said, "Do not go so quickly. Let Rebekah stay with us a few more days."

"I cannot wait," said Eliezer.

"Then we will ask Rebekah what she wishes to do," said her mother. She called to Rebekah, "Will you go with this man?"

Rebekah said, "I will go."

So Rebekah and her nurse and some servants went away with Eliezer.

Her mother blessed her, saying, "May you be happy and may God take care of you on your journey."

Rebekah and all who were with her rode on camels. After traveling a few days, they came to a field. A man stood in the center of the field with his eyes toward heaven.

"Who is that man coming toward us?" asked Rebekah.

"He is my master Isaac," said Eliezer.

Rebekah got down from her camel. When Isaac saw her, he loved her, for she was very beautiful. He took her to his mother's tent and she became his wife. Isaac and Rebekah were very happy. They had twin sons, Esau and Jacob.

Esau Sells His Birthright

A BOY stood on a cliff. A deer came out from the trees and began to nibble the sweet green grass. Then the boy took his bow and arrow and shot at the deer. He missed. The deer kicked up his hind legs and ran away.

The boy looked overhead. The sun was in the middle of the heavens.

"Why, it's noon!" cried the boy. "How hungry I am. I think I will go home and see if dinner is ready." So the boy ran down the mountain toward home. As he ran, he sang:

"I am Esau the hairy,
A hunter am I,
With my bow and arrow,
All men I defy.
Oooooai, Oooooai,
This is my cry."

34

When Esau came to his father's tent, he smelled some food cooking. There was his brother, Jacob, stirring a pot of delicious red pottage.

"What have you got there, Jacob?" he asked.

Jacob looked up and smiled. He was very different from Esau. He was a quiet boy and his skin was white and smooth.

"I've pottage red as a red berry."

"Please give me some pottage, I'm very hungry," begged Esau.

Jacob liked to tease his brother.

"Well, if you are so very hungry, you'll sell me your birthright for some of this pottage."

"No, I couldn't do that," said Esau.

You see, a birthright was a very important thing. In those days a double share of that which belonged to the father went to the oldest son when the father died. Much of Isaac's sheep, servants, and gold would belong to Esau when his father died. But more than everything else, a birthright meant that the oldest son should be leader and teacher of his family after his father's death. Esau did not care about this at all.

"What have you got there, Jacob?"

36

"No pottage for you, Esau," said Jacob.

Esau was angry. He went outside. How hot the sun was! How cool the mountains looked! He must shoot that deer he saw this morning. He was so very hungry. How good the pottage smelled! He was a hunter, he didn't need a birthright anyway. He was hungry and he wanted something to eat. So he walked into the tent and said, "Jacob, I'll sell you my birthright. Now give me some of that pottage."

Jacob filled a large bowl full of the food. Esau ate like a hungry animal.

Jacob stood in the doorway, singing:

"For a bowl of red, red pottage,
    Esau did his birthright sell,
So that Jacob is the eldest,
    And master here as well."

Esau paid no attention to his brother's song. As soon as he had finished, he let out a very loud yell and began running toward the mountains again. From the top of a hill came the cry, "Oooooai, Oooooai."

Jacob Receives the Blessing

ISAAC grew to be a very old man. His eyes became blind. He could not see. He loved his eldest son, Esau, because he was such a good hunter. Rebekah, his wife, loved Jacob, for Jacob was quiet and gentle.

One day Isaac said to Esau, "My son, I am a very old man and have not much longer to live. Go out into the woods and find a deer. Then cook the meat the way I like it. When you come back, I will bless you."

Esau took his bow and arrows and went into the woods.

Rebekah, his mother, had heard the words of Isaac. She said to herself, "Why should Esau have the blessing? He only cares to hunt and eat. Jacob is a teacher of men; he will do great things."

Then Rebekah did something that she should

38

never have done. She called, "Jacob, come here. Go out into the flock and bring me two young kids. I will cook the meat so that it will taste very good. You will take the food to your father, and he will bless you before he dies."

Jacob brought his mother the two kids. She cooked the meat the way Isaac loved it. Then she dressed Jacob in Esau's best clothing. She put the skins of goats upon his smooth hands and neck. She said, "Now take this food to your father."

Jacob went into his father's tent.

"Here I am, Father. I am Esau, your eldest son. Come, eat this meat. When you are through, you will bless me."

"How did you find the deer so quickly?" asked Isaac.

"God helped me," answered Jacob.

"Come here, my boy, that I may touch you, and see if you are really Esau."

Jacob came close to the old man. Isaac felt the boy's hands. He said, "The voice is the voice of Jacob, but the hands are the hands of Esau." The skins of the goats with which Rebekah had covered

Jacob's hands felt just like the hairy ones of his brother, Esau, so Isaac believed him. "Are you really my son Esau?" he asked again.

"I am," said Jacob.

"Then bring the meat, that I may eat."

Jacob gave his father the meat and some wine to drink.

When Isaac had finished eating, he said, "Come here, my son, and kiss me."

Jacob kissed his father. Isaac blessed him saying:

"God will give thee corn and wine,
Grassy pastures will be thine;
Thy brothers will bow down to thee,
A leader of men thou shalt be.
Cursed be he, who curseth thee,
Blessed be he, who blesseth thee."

Jacob left his father alone in his tent. Soon the old man heard the hunting song of his son Esau:

"I am Esau the hairy,
A hunter am I,
With my bow and arrow,

40

"Are you really my son, Esau?"

41

All men I defy.
Oooooai, Oooooai,
That is my cry."

Esau entered the tent with the hot food he had just cooked for his father.

"Come, my father, eat of the meat I have just cooked for you. Then you will bless me."

Isaac was surprised. "Who are you?" he cried.

"I am your oldest son, Esau."

Isaac was trembling from head to foot. "Who was it that brought me food before you came? I have already eaten and blessed the one who came before you."

When Esau heard these words, he fell on his knees before his father and cried, "Bless me also, Father, please bless me."

Isaac put his hand on the boy's head and stroked it.

"Your brother, Jacob, has fooled me. He has taken away your blessing."

Esau wept. "He has taken everything away from me. First he took my birthright, and now my bless-

"Bless me also, Father."

43

ing. Father, haven't you another blessing for me?"

"What can I say?" Isaac said sadly. "I have made Jacob a leader of men. I have given him corn and wine. What can I say to you, my son?"

Esau's face was covered with tears. "Haven't you even one blessing for me, Father? Please bless me, Father."

So Isaac held the boy's head with both his hands, and in a voice, strangely deep, he said:

"The earth to you her wealth will give,
But, Esau, by your sword you'll live.
Your brother's servant you will be,
Till one day you will shake his yoke
Forever after you'll be free."

Esau got up and left the tent without a word. He said to his mother, "When my father is dead, I will kill my brother Jacob."

Rebekah was afraid. She knew that Esau meant to do what he said. She also knew that he would be very sorry if he were to do such a thing. So she called Jacob to her and said, "Jacob, you must leave this house at once, for Esau is very angry. Go to my brother Laban's house. When Esau has forgiven you, I will send for you to come back."

Jacob packed up his belongings and set out upon his journey. Before he left, he went into his father's tent to say goodby.

Isaac said, "God bless you, my son, and may you find a wife among the daughters of Laban."

So Jacob left his father's house and began the long journey to Paddan-Aram, the land in which his uncle Laban lived.

So the blessing which Jacob obtained by deceiving his father did not help him. He had to leave his father and his mother and go far away from home, a lonely wanderer, into a far-off land.

Jacob Dreams

JACOB traveled until he came to a wood. As he looked up in the sky, he saw the setting sun. Night was coming on, and he was very tired.

He looked about him on the ground for a place where he might rest for the night. There he saw a large flat stone.

He said, "This stone shall be my pillow and this soft green grass my bed."

He lay down with his head on the rock and soon was fast asleep.

Just as he closed his eyes, the woods became bright. Jacob sat up and looked around. A short distance away was a ladder which reached from the earth to heaven. Angels were running up and down the ladder. They made a circle around Jacob.

They picked up the soil upon which he was lying and sang:

"To Jacob all this soil belongs,
His children, forming mighty throngs,
Will spread to east, south, north, and west,
And Jacob's children will be blessed."

Then Jacob heard the voice of God, saying, "Jacob, I give you this land, and no matter where you go I will be with you."

The angels walked up the ladder into heaven and were gone.

Jacob woke up. It was broad daylight. He said, "God has been in this place and I did not know it. Surely God is with me no matter where I am."

Then Jacob took the stone which he had used as a pillow and poured oil over it. "Now I have made this stone holy. I shall call this place Bethel, which means 'House of God.'"

Jacob went on his journey with happiness in his heart.

Jacob Wins Rachel

HAVE you ever seen a flock of sheep huddled together in the center of a field? They look like snowdrifts in winter, so white and downy are their backs. This was the sight Jacob saw when he came into the land of the children of the east.

Two shepherds were drawing water from a large well which stood under a tree. The well was covered with a huge stone, which the men had to roll back and forth in order to draw the water. Jacob came up and spoke to the men. He said, "Who are you?"

"We are men of the east," they answered.

"Do you know of a man called Laban?" Jacob asked.

"Yes, we know him. Here comes his daughter Rachel with his sheep."

Jacob saw a young girl driving a flock of sheep

toward the well. He had never seen such a beautiful girl before. She had the same dark hair and sparkling eyes as his mother, Rebekah. When she smiled, it was as if two rows of pearls shone from her mouth. Jacob loved her from the very first moment that he saw her.

Turning to the shepherds, he said, "Let me watch the well for a while. I will see that the stone is rolled back over the well."

The shepherds went away leaving Jacob alone at the well. When Rachel came to the well, she was surprised to see Jacob there. He was very different from the young men of the east. He was so gentle and his skin was so smooth and fair.

Jacob said, "Fairest daughter of the east, I will water your flocks."

He drew water for all the sheep of Laban's flock. When Rachel came near the well he kissed her. Rachel was half surprised and half pleased at this strange young man. She said, "Who are you, stranger? Where did you come from?"

Jacob said, "I am your cousin Jacob. My mother, Rebekah, is a sister to your father, Laban."

Rachel laughed. "So you are my cousin Jacob. Wait here. I will tell my father you are here."

Rachel ran and told her father of the young man at the well. When Laban heard that Jacob was at the well, he came to meet him. He kissed Jacob, saying, "You are like my own son; come and stay with us for a while."

Jacob stayed in Laban's house. He helped Rachel with the sheep. Every day he grew to love her more.

One day Laban said, "You have been here a month, Jacob. You work very hard. It is not right that you work for nothing. What do you want for wages?"

"I do not want wages, Laban; I want Rachel, your youngest daughter, for my wife. I will work without wages for seven years if you will give her to me."

"Very well," answered Laban. "It is better that I give her to you than to a man I do not know."

For seven years Jacob worked very hard. He loved Rachel so much that the time seemed like a few days. When the seven years had passed, he said to Laban, "Give me your daughter Rachel as you promised."

"You have fooled me, Laban."

Now Laban had two daughters. Leah, the oldest, was not as pretty a girl as Rachel. Since she was not married, Laban thought that she should have a husband first. So he made a large feast and invited the people from all the country around. When Jacob was married, his bride had a heavy veil over her face. Imagine his surprise when the bride took off her veil and he saw that she was Leah instead of Rachel!

"You have fooled me, Laban," he cried out. "I worked seven long years for Rachel and not Leah."

"It is not the custom of this country for the younger to be married first. If you really want Rachel, work another seven years, and I will give her to you."

For seven more years Jacob worked for Laban. Then Rachel became his wife and he loved her greatly. Rachel and Jacob had a son called Joseph.

Jacob Is Named Israel

FOR twenty years Jacob worked for Laban. During those years he grew very rich, for he had large herds of sheep and goats. He also had eleven sons and daughters.

One day he said to Laban, "I have lived here long enough. I want to go back to the land of my father, Isaac." He called together all his wives, children, and his servants and said, "Round up the cattle and pack the household goods for we are going back to the land of my fathers."

Jacob could not help but wonder how Esau would treat him after so many years. He sent messengers ahead to meet Esau. Jacob said, "Tell my brother Esau that I have lived with Laban all these years; that I have many herds of sheep and many servants. Tell him that I wish to find favor in his sight."

The servants went on ahead as Jacob had told

them. But they soon returned. "Did you see my brother Esau?" asked Jacob.

"Yes, we have seen him," they answered. "He is coming to meet you with four hundred men."

"Four hundred men!" cried Jacob. "I shall divide my people into two camps. If Esau attacks one camp, the other will be saved."

Jacob divided his people into two camps, but he was very much afraid. That night he prayed to God. "Oh, God, save me from the anger of my brother Esau for I fear he will kill all of my people."

Then he took the finest sheep and goats of his flock and gave them to the same two servants, saying, "Take these animals to Esau as presents from me. Tell him that I am coming to meet him."

Jacob watched the servants leave with the gifts. Then he ordered camp to be made. He would pass the night in that place waiting for Esau.

The last of the camp fires had died down. Only the moon lighted the field. Jacob stood on the other side of the stream alone. He could not sleep. "Oh, why can't I sleep?" he cried. "I shall cross the stream and find rest inside the camp."

"You shall not leave this spot." A voice out of the darkness frightened him. A shadow-like man stood by his side.

"Who are you?" Jacob called.

"I have hold of you, and you cannot get away."

"Let me go," Jacob shouted, for the man had grasped him around his waist.

"You shall never go," the man said, holding Jacob tighter.

Then Jacob began to wrestle with the man. All night they fought. The man would throw Jacob to the ground with such force that it seemed he would never get up. Then Jacob would stand up again. He would grasp the man again and again and begin the fight all over.

The moon looked down and said:

"I'll give light,
Jacob fight,
For your might,
Through the night."

The wind blew the branches of the trees and sang, "Ou, Ou, Ou."

Jacob seemed to gain strength. Night had almost ended. The sky was gray with the coming of dawn. Jacob had hold of the man.

"Let me go," cried the man, "for the day is here."

"I will not let you go till you bless me," cried Jacob.

"What is your name?"

"Jacob."

"Your name is no longer Jacob," said the man, "for you have fought with both God and man, and you have won. From now on your name is Israel. I bless you, Israel."

"Who are you?" cried Jacob. He shouted and clutched at the air for the man had gone.

And Jacob fell upon the ground and prayed.

Esau Forgives Jacob

THE next morning the air was thick with dust. The earth shook from the noise of the hoofs of Esau's four hundred horsemen. Esau rode at their head. He was very dark, his hair and beard were long, and his deep-set eyes gleamed like two small stars.

"Halt!" he cried suddenly. Esau's men came to a stop. A short distance away stood Jacob's camp. Esau knew his brother Jacob, who stood there to meet him. But he was surprised to see so many people.

First came the servants with all their children. Then Leah and her six sons. In back of Leah was Rachel with her son Joseph. Jacob was walking toward Esau. As he came he bowed seven times.

Esau got down off his horse and ran to meet Jacob. He took his brother in his arms and kissed

They wept with joy at seeing each other again.

him. The two brothers wept with joy at seeing each other again.

Esau said, "Who are all these people with you?"

"They are the children whom God has given me."

All the servants bowed to Esau. Leah and her sons bowed to Esau. Then Rachel and Joseph came up to Esau and bowed down.

Esau was overcome. "Why have you brought your entire camp here, Jacob?"

"To find favor in your eyes."

"My brother, I have plenty of animals. You shouldn't give me the best of your flock."

"I have seen in your face that you are pleased with me, Esau. Please take my gifts," answered Jacob.

So Esau took the gifts and said, "Let us go on the rest of the journey together." Esau led the way and Jacob followed with all his household. Jacob came into the land of Canaan. There he decided to live as did his father before him.

What Joseph Dreamt

JACOB settled in the land of Canaan. As you know, Jacob had twelve sons and one daughter. Jacob loved all his children, but the one he loved the best was called Joseph.

Now Joseph and his brothers were shepherds. They all wore brown sheepskin coats and carried staffs. One day Jacob gave Joseph a beautiful coat made of silk. There were so many different colors in the coat that it looked like a rainbow. Sometimes it was red, green, and violet; other times, it was yellow, orange, and blue. When the brothers saw this coat, they were angry and said, "Why should Joseph wear a coat of many colors, while we must wear these ugly, brown sheepskin coats?"

The brothers began to dislike Joseph. They not only disliked him because of his coat, but because he was always telling them of his strange dreams. One

60

night Joseph had such a queer dream that, instead of laughing at him, the brothers became very angry. This is the dream that Joseph told:

Joseph dreamed that he was out in the fields. A large, round moon was shining down on him. Suddenly all his brothers came dancing in. They danced in and out of the wheat, cutting it down as they danced. After all the wheat had been cut, they began to bind it into sheaves. Joseph made a sheaf, too, but it was bigger than all the rest. The brothers sang:

"Joseph's sheaf is the best,
Better wheat than all the rest;
Joseph's sheaf is the best,
Better wheat than all the rest."

When the brothers sang this song, all the sheaves of wheat began to move. The sheaves formed a circle around Joseph's sheaf, singing this song:

"Let us bow to Joseph's sheaf,
It is bigger, better wheat;
Let us bow to Joseph's sheaf,
It is best of all to eat."

61

"Let us bow to Joseph's sheaf."

All the sheaves bowed down to Joseph's sheaf, while the brothers kept on singing their song. Then Joseph woke up.

When Joseph told his brothers this dream, they cried, "We suppose your dream means that we shall bow down to you? That you will rule over us?"

Joseph answered, "I just told you my dream; I cannot tell you what it means."

The brothers answered, "Yes, you think you will rule over us, but you won't. We don't believe your silly dream."

Joseph did not like to have his brothers angry with him, yet the next night he had an even stranger dream.

Joseph dreamed he was up in the sky. It was night. He walked on the clouds just as if they made a black carpet. All about him were stars. There were big stars, little stars, tiny stars.

Three of the tiniest stars brought Joseph a golden throne. The throne shone so brightly that Joseph thought it was made of gold. When he sat down on the throne, he saw that it was made of tiny little stars.

Just as Joseph seated himself, eleven of the largest stars in the sky came up to his throne and bowing down to him, sang:

"Let us bow to Joseph,
All stars in the sky;
Let us bow to Joseph,
For he sits so high."

The big stars then marched in a line behind

The stars bow to Joseph.

63

Joseph's throne. Joseph saw a beautiful yellow light
in the distance. It looked as if a lady were in the light.
When the light came closer, he saw that it was the
moon. The moon bowed down to him, just as the
stars had done, and the moon sang:

"Down to Joseph bows the moon,
All the sky will bow down soon;
Down to Joseph bows the moon,
Come, you stars, and sing this tune."

The stars began to bow and sing the same song.
The sky became light as day. Joseph had to close his
eyes at this sudden light. When he opened them, he
saw a large, golden ball bowing before him. This ball
cast off rays so bright that Joseph knew that the sun
was bowing to him. For a moment he was afraid that
the sun had come to burn him up. The sun began to
sing:

"The sun bows down to Joseph
The sun gives heat and light;
The sun bows down to Joseph
Till day is changed to night."

64

Now everything in the sky was bowing, sun, moon, and stars. The stars began to dance. The sky became so light, Joseph could not see. He was in a whirl of light. He was tumbling out of his throne. Down, down, down, Joseph was falling through the sky. A great big star came sailing by. Joseph caught hold of its tail. The star gave a jerk, and Joseph lost his hold. Down, down, down! Would he never stop falling? At last he saw the earth beneath him. Then, bump! Joseph opened his eyes. He was in his own house. He had fallen out of bed.

Joseph caught hold of its tail.

Joseph Is Sold into Slavery

THE sun was smiling through the rain as it sometimes does after a summer rain. Joseph's brothers,
who were watching the sheep, looked to the top of
a little hill and cried, "Look! A rainbow!"

But they did not see a rainbow, for the rainbow
was moving toward them. It was young Joseph in his
coat of many colors.

"The dreamer is coming!" said one of them.

"Our father gives him a beautiful coat and listens
to his silly dreams, while we have to work in the
fields," said a second.

"Come, let's throw him into one of the pits
around here, and kill him," said a third.

"What will our father think if we do such a terrible thing?" said Reuben.

"We will tell him a wild beast ate Joseph up," said
the third.

Then the brothers laughed. "A fine dreamer he'll be when we are through with him!"

"Stop your silly laughing," cried Reuben. "We will not kill Joseph. If you must be rid of him, leave him in one of the pits alone in the wilderness."

Reuben was not like the other brothers. He loved Joseph and he planned to save Joseph when his brothers had gone away.

Joseph had now come near the flock. His brothers took hold of him and tore the beautiful coat from his back. They threw him into a pit which had no water in it. Then they sat around the edge of the pit laughing at poor Joseph.

They even began to eat bread, for it was noon. Poor Joseph crawled in the pit. He was so hungry. The big empty pit frightened him so.

Soon they heard a noise. In the distance was a caravan, a long train of people riding on camels. The camels were loaded down with spices and perfumes which were to be taken to Egypt.

"A caravan!" cried another brother, Judah. All the brothers stood up and began shouting at the top of their voices, "A caravan! A caravan!"

Joseph looked back at his cruel brothers.

"I have an idea," said Judah. "We will not gain anything by killing Joseph, for after all he is our brother. Let us sell him to these merchants."

This was agreeable to the brothers. They stopped the caravan as it passed by.

A tall Ishmaelite came up to them. "What do you want?"

"We have a boy here, a Hebrew slave. What will you give us for him?"

The merchant looked at the boy in the pit. "Twenty pieces of silver."

"Take him," the brothers called out.

The merchant lifted Joseph out of the pit. He put him on the back of a camel and soon they were on their way across the wilderness.

Joseph looked back at his cruel brothers.

Reuben had been tending sheep when his brothers had sold Joseph to the merchants.

When he came back and did not find the boy in the pit, he cried, "What have you done with my brother Joseph? Oh, what will become of me, now that Joseph is gone?" He ran about calling, "Joseph! Joseph!"

Then one of the brothers who had killed a goat and rubbed Joseph's coat in the blood said, "This is what became of Joseph—a wild beast ate him up."

Reuben wept. He took the bloody coat to his father, Jacob.

When Jacob saw the coat he wept. No one could comfort him. He said, "I have lost my child. No one can ever comfort me."

Joseph Is Sent to Prison

Many years later Joseph stood outside of his master's house looking at the country he had now come to call his own. How different from the wilderness of Canaan! Instead of rugged mountains and empty plains, there were well-watered fields of corn. There were beautiful palaces where the king lived. There were temples and strange gods. Then there was the desert with those huge triangles of solid stone called the pyramids.

Joseph was master now. The merchants had sold him to Potiphar, the captain of the king's guard. Within a few years he had risen from a common servant to master of Potiphar's house. Egypt was a wonderful land, but he often longed for the wilderness of Canaan. He longed to see his father, Jacob, and his younger brother, Benjamin. Tears came to his eyes, for he was so lonely here.

"I will throw you into prison!"

He did not hear the wife of Potiphar coming toward him.

"Dreaming as usual," she said.

Joseph was startled. He turned to see the wife of his master. He bowed low and smiled at her.

Potiphar's wife was a beautiful woman, but she was selfish and her eyes were cruel.

Joseph did not like Potiphar's wife. He always treated her politely, but he would never say much to her. This made her angry. She wanted to make Potiphar dislike Joseph. So she said, "Is this all you have to do, idle your time away?"

"I am not idling away my time. My work is well done; my master is pleased."

"I am not pleased," she cried out in anger. "I shall tell my husband how lazy you are, and he shall throw you into prison for the way you spoke to me."

Joseph did not answer but walked away from the cruel woman.

That evening when her husband came home, she told him that Joseph was lazy.

Potiphar called Joseph to him. "Who are you to be rude to my wife? You, whom I took in as a slave

73

and made master of my house! I will throw you into prison."

Joseph tried to tell Potiphar of the lies his wife told. But Potiphar only became angrier. He called the guard. They tied Joseph with strong ropes and threw him into prison with the rest of the king's prisoners.

The keeper of the prison knew that Joseph was not to blame. He untied Joseph and made Joseph guard over all the other prisoners. Joseph thanked the keeper, but he also thanked God. He knew that God had made the heart of the keeper of the prison kindly toward him.

Joseph in Prison

THERE were two new prisoners. They were rather grand prisoners, these two. One was very thin and always worried about the curl in his hair. He was the Pharaoh's chief butler. The other was very large and fat. He was the Pharaoh's chief baker. They were always talking and making a lot of noise. One morning they were very silent and sad looking.

"Why are you so sad?" asked Joseph.

"We had such strange dreams last night. Nobody can tell us what they mean."

"What were your dreams?" asked Joseph.

The chief butler said:

"A vine with branches three,
With grapes hung low for me.
In Pharaoh's cup the grapes I pressed,
The cup he took and then me blessed."

"In Pharaoh's cup the grapes I pressed."

Joseph smiled and said:

"Three days are meant by branches three,
Within three days again you'll be
The Pharaoh's butler,
And wine to him again you'll serve.
But when again you've freedom gained,
Remember me in prison chained.
For I come from a land that's free,
I was not brought here rightfully."

The chief butler wondered at Joseph's explanation of his dream.

The chief baker said, "Now tell me the meaning of my dream. It was like this:

"I held on my head,
Three baskets of bread,
There was food
Hot and good,
But birds came to eat
The bread and the meat."

Joseph answered:
"The baskets are three days,
Pharaoh will punish thy evil ways.

"But birds came to eat."

Three days after Joseph had told them the meaning of their dreams, the Pharaoh had a birthday. He made a great feast. The baker, who was a very wicked man, was hanged, but the butler was freed from prison. Once again he was waiting on the Pharaoh. But no sooner was he out of prison than the butler forgot all about Joseph.

Joseph Explains Pharaoh's Dreams

T WO years passed by. Joseph was still in prison. One day the keeper of the prison came to Joseph and said:

"Shave yourself and put on these rich clothes. The Pharaoh commands you to come to the Palace."

Joseph was so surprised he could hardly believe the man's words. After two long years in prison he was at last to be freed. He quickly dressed himself in the beautiful clothing.

Two soldiers brought him before the Pharaoh.

Pharaoh said, "My butler has told me that you can tell the meaning of dreams. Is that true?"

"Yes," answered Joseph.

"Be careful what you say, young man, for I have called in all the magicians in the land of Egypt, and none of them can tell me the meaning of my dreams."

Joseph was fearless.

80

Joseph was fearless. "Tell me your dreams, great Pharaoh. God has given me the power to tell the meaning of dreams."

The Pharaoh said:

"I was sitting by the river Nile. The river was peaceful and green. Suddenly seven cows came out of the river. They walked out of the water one behind the other, and they sang this song:

" 'We are fat cows large and brown,
We give milk and we give meat;
We feed all within this land
When we're here there's much to eat.'

"These cows started to eat the tall green grass which grows by the river.

"Then the river turned black and flowed swiftly. Out of the river came seven more cows. They were so thin that their bones stood out of their bodies like mountain ridges.

"They sang this song:

" 'We are hungry; give us grain,
We will eat in sun and rain,

And the land of food we'll drain,
  Then no corn will grow again.'

"The thin cows began to eat up the grass by the river. When that was gone, they ate up the seven fat cows.

"But that is not all, for the next night I had another dream.

"I was in the middle of a field. Suddenly there sprang up seven ears of corn. Such beautiful ears of corn they were! They were large and golden. The corn swayed back and forth in the wind and sang this song:

" 'Ears of corn so golden,
    Ears of corn so good,
  Grown from soil so fertile,
    Corn the finest food.'

"Then the air was hot. The wind began to blow. Up sprang seven more ears of corn! But this corn was withered and hard. It was not fit to eat. This corn walked about in a circle and said:

" 'From the poorest soil this corn does **grow**,
    No man or beast we feed;
      But ever growing row on row,
        To rot and go to seed.'

"The bad ears of corn began to dance around the good corn. The wind blew and the air became hotter and hotter. Faster and faster danced the bad ears of corn. Then they swooped down on the good ears of corn and ate them all up.

"What does this dream mean, young man?"
Joseph answered:

"The seven good cows are seven good years,
    The seven good corn are seven good years;
    The seven bad cows are seven bad years,
    The seven bad corn are seven bad years.
    For seven years this land will see,
    Good crops, large herds, prosperity.
    And then a famine down will swoop,
    The cows will die, the corn will droop,
    And you, O Pharaoh, wise and grand,
    Will find a man in Egypt's land,

To store up plenty of corn and meat,
So Egypt will not starve, but eat."

Pharaoh answered, "You have spoken with great wisdom. Since God has shown you what to do in case of famine, I will make you head of the land of Egypt. Here, take my signet ring, so that you may know that I believe in you."

Joseph took the ring. He was dressed in the finest clothing and was given a beautiful horse and chariot. He was lord in the land of Egypt.

The Pharaoh's dreams came true. There were seven years of plenty. The crops were better than ever before. During this time Joseph had huge houses built. In these he stored grain. For the time was soon coming when famine would enter the land.

Joseph Meets His Brothers Again

FAMINE had spread itself all over the face of the earth. No food would grow in the fields, for the hot sun would burn it up, or too much rain would make it rot. Everywhere people were dying of hunger. Even in the land of Canaan where Jacob lived with his sons there was famine.

The famine became so bad that soon there was not a grain of corn to eat. Jacob said to his sons, "Why do you stay here and do nothing? I have heard that there is plenty of corn in Egypt. Go down to Egypt and buy some of their corn. If you do not, we will all die." All the sons went down into Egypt, except Benjamin. Jacob was afraid to let Benjamin go for he was the youngest, and he feared that he would die as Joseph was supposed to have died.

Joseph was now ruler of Egypt. People from all the surrounding countries came to Egypt to buy

"Where are you from?"

86

grain from him. One day a servant came to him and said, "My lord, there are ten Hebrews who wish to buy corn."

"Let them come in," said Joseph. He was eager to see these men, for he thought they might be his brothers. The men came in very humbly. They bowed so low that their faces touched the ground. As soon as Joseph saw them, he knew they were his brothers. His heart began to beat violently.

He said in a rough voice, "Where are you from?"

"We come from the land of Canaan to buy food," they answered.

Joseph knew that his brothers did not know him. He remembered the dream he had as a boy, the dream that had caused him to be sold into slavery. So he said, "You are spies. You have come to see how we suffer from famine in this land."

"We are not spies. We have only come for food. We starve in the land of Canaan. We are twelve brothers, the sons of one man in Canaan. Our youngest brother is at home with our father."

"Then if you are not spies," said Joseph, "you will bring your youngest brother here to me, and while you are gone one of you will be kept in prison till you return."

The brothers were afraid. They left one of their brothers with Joseph. Then Joseph ordered their sacks to be filled full of corn. The brothers went back to Canaan. When they came home and opened their sacks, what should they find but the money they had given Joseph for the corn at the top of their sacks.

The brothers were more afraid than before. "Now the man will think we really are spies, for he will surely think that we have stolen this money. Let us take Benjamin back to him, or he will be angry with us."

"No," cried Jacob. "Benjamin will not go with you. Is it not enough that I have lost my other son, Joseph?"

The brothers did not go back to Egypt for some time. But the famine became worse.

Soon all the corn was eaten up, and Jacob cried out, "We must have something to eat. Go down to Egypt and buy some more corn."

"We dare not go back without Benjamin, or the

man will give us nothing," answered the sons.

Jacob could see that there was nothing else to do, so he said, "Very well, take the boy. But take double the amount of money. Perhaps the man will be kind to the boy."

So Jacob's sons went down into Egypt again. They went before Joseph. They put the boy Benjamin in front of them, saying, "Here is our youngest brother."

When Joseph saw his little brother, he wanted to rush forward and kiss him, for he loved the boy dearly. He was filled with joy. That no one might see him he went into another room and wept. He was not yet ready to tell his brothers who he was.

The brothers were taken into Joseph's house and given a meal of the finest food in Egypt. All were given gifts but Benjamin received five times as many as the other brothers, for that was Joseph's wish.

Joseph said to one of his servants, "Fill the men's sacks with as much food as they can carry. Also put their money in the sacks. But in the sack of the youngest boy put my silver cup."

The next morning the brothers set out for Canaan.

Joseph said to his servant, "Follow these men. Search all their sacks until you find my silver cup. Then bring the men back to me."

The brothers were well on their way home when they heard the voices of Joseph's servants who cried, "Stop!"

"What do you want with us?" cried Judah, the strongest.

The servant said, "Is it not enough that our master has given you corn and money? Now you steal his silver cup from his house!"

"We have no silver cup. If the cup is found, we shall be your servants," cried the brothers.

"We will search your sacks and see for ourselves," said the servants.

The servants searched all the sacks and in the sack of Benjamin, the youngest, they found the silver cup. So all the brothers had to turn back to Joseph's house. When they came before Joseph, they fell to the ground. Joseph said, "Why did you do such a thing? Didn't you know I would find you out?"

The brothers wept and said, "What can we do to prove that we did not steal the cup?"

"Give me the one in whose sack the cup was found."

Joseph answered, "Give me the one in whose sack the cup was found as my servant." Joseph thought in this way he would keep his brother Benjamin near him.

But Judah came forward and said, "Do not take the boy. It would kill our father if we did not bring him home with us. He is a very old man and has had much sorrow in his life. He lost another son and has never stopped mourning for him. Can't you take any of us but Benjamin for your servant?"

When Joseph heard these words, he commanded his servants, "Leave me alone with these men." Joseph's eyes filled with tears. "I am Joseph, your brother. Is my father still living?"

The brothers were afraid of this great man. "Do not be afraid," said Joseph. "I am Joseph, your brother. You sold me as a slave to the merchants. But God watched over me. He has made me ruler over the land of Egypt." Then he took his brother Benjamin in his arms and kissed him. He kissed all his brothers and wept with joy at seeing them.

Then they sat together and talked. Joseph said, "Tell my father that I am alive. Tell him that I am lord over all of Egypt. Since there are five more years of famine, take my father and all your families and herds of cattle and come into Egypt to live."

The brothers promised to do this. Joseph gave them gifts, but to Benjamin he gave fine clothes and silver. So the brothers went back to Canaan. They said to their father, "Joseph is still living; he is ruler of the land of Egypt."

Jacob almost fainted when he heard these words. Then his sons told him of all that had happened and showed the gifts Joseph had given them.

Jacob felt young again. "Joseph, my son, is alive! I will go and see him before I die."

Jacob Settles in Egypt

~∞~

JACOB gathered together all his household goods and journeyed into Egypt. Joseph came to meet him in a beautiful chariot. When Joseph saw his father, he embraced and kissed him and wept with joy at seeing him again.

Joseph went before the Pharaoh and said, "My father and twelve brothers have left the land of Canaan. They are living in the land of Goshen. Will you allow them to live in this land?"

"What is their occupation?" asked Pharaoh.

"They are shepherds," answered Joseph.

"You have done much for Egypt, Joseph. Let your family settle in the most fertile part of Egypt." So Jacob and his twelve sons settled in the land of Goshen.

Jacob was getting very old. Before he died he called all his sons together. He blessed each one.

Each son was the father of a tribe. From them came the twelve tribes of Israel.

When Jacob died, they buried him in the land of Canaan, for that was his wish.

Joseph lived to be a very old man. He was one hundred and ten years old when he died. He was very much loved not only by his own people, but by the Egyptians as well.

The Birth of Moses

MANY years passed, and a new Pharaoh came to rule the land of Egypt. He was very cruel to the Hebrews. He made them work very hard. They built great stone cities, pulling heavy stones from miles around. The Hebrews were very sad. They cried, "Why must we work so hard? Oh, great Pharaoh, have you no pity for us?"

Instead of listening to their pleas the cruel Pharaoh said, "These Hebrews must die or soon there will be more Hebrews than Egyptians. From this hour on, every Hebrew boy that is born will be thrown into the Nile."

No sooner had the Pharaoh given this command, than a Hebrew baby boy was born. This boy was the son of a man of the tribe of Levi, called Amram. His mother was called Jochebed.

Amram and his wife had been very happy. They

had two other children, the eldest, a boy named Aaron, the other, a girl named Miriam. They were very poor, and their little house was almost empty. Yet when Amram came home from hard work, he loved to tell the children about the happy land of their ancestors, of Abraham and Isaac, of Joseph, and all that he did for Egypt. He would say, "Some day God will take us out of all this misery. Perhaps you, my children, will see this wonderful land."

The people said, "Poor Amram! His beautiful son will be thrown into the Nile. Let us go to his house and tell him of the Pharaoh's command."

The people wept, for they were sorry for Amram, but when they came to his house, they suddenly became filled with joy. The sun cast tiny sunbeams about the house, making it shine like a beautiful star, and the mother, Jochebed, held in her arms the most beautiful baby boy they had ever seen.

Jochebed said, "The Egyptians need not know that this child has been born. I will hide him. None of our people will tell them."

So for three months they hid the baby safely. Like all healthy babies he was perfectly content to eat and sleep. But soon the baby began to try to sit up. He tried to talk, and cried in a loud voice.

One day Jochebed took the baby outside for some air. Aaron and Miriam were playing nearby. Tramp! tramp! tramp! Some Egyptian soldiers were coming toward them.

"Quick, mother, hide the baby! The soldiers are coming! They are searching all the houses for children."

Jochebed ran into the house. She hid the baby under some clothing. The baby was sound asleep and did not make any noise. The soldiers came into the house. They cared for nothing. They upset everything in the house. When they did not find what they were looking for, they stamped out of the house slamming the door after them.

When Amram came home, he found Jochebed, Miriam, and Aaron all weeping bitterly.

"What is the matter?" he cried.

"The soldiers have come at last, Amram," said Jochebed. "This time I was able to hide the baby because he was asleep. They will find him sooner or later."

The soldiers upset everything in the house.

Amram tried to comfort her, but Jochebed could only weep. At last she dried her tears.

Jochebed took some straw and began to weave a basket. Amram watched her nimble fingers fashion a basket out of the straw. All night she worked. When the basket was finished, she said, "Here, Amram, paint this basket all over with tar. I am going to put the baby in the river myself. Perhaps some kind person will find him and take pity on him."

The next morning Miriam followed closely behind her mother, and she carried the baby to the river. The day was so beautiful. The birds were singing and lovely flowers grew by the river's banks.

Jochebed placed the basket in some tall bulrushes. The bulrushes held the basket safely. Jochebed kissed the sleeping boy tenderly, then went off a short distance to see what would happen.

The water sang:

> "Sweet little baby,
>   With little pink feet,
> Softly we rock you,
>   And soon you will sleep."

The Princess

A SHORT distance up the river stood the Pharaoh's palace. "Splash! Splash!" said the waves as they washed against the palace walls. "When is the Princess coming for her bath?"

Ten beautiful Egyptian maidens stood waving palm boughs. They sang this song:

"Hail to the Princess,
Fair as the sun;
Queen of the Earth,
Queen of the Nile,
Hail to the Princess,
Fair as the sun."

Two black slaves carried the Princess in a litter. She was wrapped in cloth as green as the waves. Her lovely long hair shone in the sunshine. But the Princess was not happy, for she cried in an angry voice, "Stop singing! I get so tired of the same thing day after day. I will not bathe here today."

"But Princess!" cried all the maidens, who were very shocked.

"No, I am going to bathe farther down the river, where the bulrushes grow. Carry me to the place where the bulrushes grow."

The two black slaves picked up the litter and the maidens followed after them singing this song:

"By the banks of the river
Tall bulrushes grow.
They'll hide our Princess
As a-bathing she'll go."

When they came to the bulrushes, the Princess stepped out of the litter and began running up and down the bank. She was delighted with the lovely flowers which grew near the river. Then she put her little feet into the water to see if it was cold. She waded out into the stream. Suddenly she cried, "Oh! oh!" She seemed to hear a low cry. She began to look among the bulrushes. The slaves dived into the water, for they thought that she was hurt. Instead she came out of the river laughing. In her arms was a basket, and from the basket came a noise like the cry of a baby.

"Look what I have found!" she cried.

The maids crowded around her. "Why, it's a baby," they all cried together.

"Poor little thing, he's crying," said the Princess. "I must have frightened him."

"Where do you suppose he came from?" asked the maids.

"He must belong to some Hebrew mother who could not bear to see him drowned. How happy I am to have found him! But who will take care of the baby?"

As if in answer to her question, Miriam appeared. She said, "I saw you find the baby, Princess. See, he is crying very hard. I know of a Hebrew woman who will nurse him for you."

The Princess was pleased. "Why, that is just what the baby needs. Run and get the woman as quickly as you can."

Miriam ran right over to her mother and told her that the Princess wished to see her. When Jochebed came before the Princess, she bowed very low.

"What is your name, young woman?" asked the Princess.

"Jochebed."

"Take this child and nurse it. I will give you wages."

Jochebed took the child in her arms and kissed it. Both she and Miriam were so happy they could hardly speak. The Princess was happy, too. She said, "I will make the boy my son. I will call him Moses, because I drew him out of the water."

Moses Fights for the Weak

T HE moon cast its light upon the wall which surrounded the Pharaoh's palace. The shadow of a woman walked back and forth as though waiting for someone.

It was Jochebed. Many years had passed since the Princess had found Moses in the bulrushes. Jochebed was now an old woman.

A voice cried out of the darkness, "Mother, Jochebed, are you there?"

Jochebed came out into the moonlight. She cried, "Moses! My son, where have you been?"

"Be quiet! No one must know I am here. If they find me, they will kill me."

"What is the matter, Moses? You are a Prince of Egypt. No one would dare to kill you."

"The Pharaoh will kill me, for I have done an awful thing. I have killed a man."

105

"Leave the slave alone!"

106

Jochebed turned pale. "How did it happen, Moses?"

"Today I went to see the store cities of Pithom and Rameses. I never knew that human beings could be so low. To see those poor Hebrew slaves hauling stones and doing work lower than that of animals was more than I could stand. There was one poor slave who was so tired he could stand no longer. He stopped to rest a moment. An Egyptian came up to him and cried, 'Slave of a Hebrew, this is no place for rest. Work, I tell you, work!' He struck the Hebrew in the face with a whip. The poor slave fell to the ground bleeding. I couldn't stand the sight of such cruelty, Mother. I grabbed the whip out of the Egyptian's hand and cried, 'Leave the slave alone. Have you no pity for him?'

" 'Give me back my whip!' he cried, in an angry voice. Then he tried to take it from me. The next thing I knew, I was beating the Egyptian, and he was dead at my feet.

" 'Hide him! Hide him in the sand!' cried the Hebrew. 'No one but you and I know what has happened.'

"I hid the Egyptian in the sand. For days I wandered about, afraid that everyone knew what I had done. One morning I came upon two Hebrews fighting. I said, 'Why are you fighting?'

"They turned to me and said, 'Who made you a judge over us? Are you going to kill us as you killed the Egyptian?'

"I ran away, for I knew my guilt was known and that I must go away. I have waited for darkness to hide me, Mother, that I may say goodby to you."

Jochebed was weeping. "It is best that you go away, but always remember that you are a Hebrew. God must have sent the Princess to find you and rear you as a Prince of Egypt. All these years I have hoped that you would be a leader of men. Always remember that the slaves, the poor people in Egypt, are your people, Moses. You are one of them; you must help them."

Moses fell at his mother's feet and wept.

Then he kissed her and left, saying, "I shall never forget the suffering of my people, dear Mother. I shall do what I can to lead them out of slavery."

He was gone.

As the dawn came up, Jochebed's lonely figure could still be seen outlined against the sky. She was looking far off into the wilderness for her son Moses.

Moses Becomes a Shepherd

IT WAS evening and the shepherds of Midian were coming to the well to water their flocks. What a raggedy lot they were! Their bodies were covered with sheepskins and their hair hung in strings about their sunburned faces.

"Look!" cried the leader. "The daughters of Jethro, the priest, have come to the well before us."

"Let us scare them away," said a second shepherd. "Let us make a terrible noise so the dogs will bark. These girls are afraid of dogs."

The shepherds began to shout at the top of their voices, "Ooohai! Oooai! Make way, make way!"

"Bow wow! Bow wow!" barked the dogs.

"Baa! Baa!" bleated the sheep.

What a frightful noise it was! The daughters of the priest, Jethro, were so frightened they did not know what to do.

Suddenly a large, dark man appeared. It was Moses.

"Stop that noise," he cried to the shepherds. "Leave the girls alone."

The shepherds stopped shouting. They were afraid of the stranger. One of the bolder shepherds said, "Who are you to tell us to go away?"

Moses looked at them steadily and said, "Go away, I tell you."

He looked so stern that the shepherds went away. Then Moses said to the girls, "Come close to the well. I will water the sheep for you."

One of the girls came forward. Her name was Zipporah. She said:

"Thank you, stranger,
My father I'll tell,
How you drove the shepherds
Away from the well."

She ran off toward home while Moses watered all the sheep.

Soon Zipporah came back with an old man. He said, "I am Jethro, Priest of Midian. Are you the

Egyptian who drove the shepherds away from the well?"

Moses smiled and nodded.

"Come home with me," said the old man. "I will give you something to eat and a place to rest."

Moses had been wandering for days. He was tired and hungry. He went home with the priest. He stayed with him and became a shepherd.

Zipporah was the most beautiful of all Jethro's daughters. Moses loved her very much, so Jethro gave her to Moses as his wife.

For seven years Moses was a shepherd. He was very happy. He and Zipporah had a son called Gershom.

The Burning Bush

THE thorn bush was the ugliest of all the trees in the wilderness. The other trees had large leaves and towered high toward heaven. But the thorn bush was small and had sharp thorns for leaves.

All the trees looked down on the thorn bush.

"Thorn bush, you are so lowly. Birds do not build nests in your branches. You do not bear fruit. Man does not use your wood for building homes. You are only an ugly bush with ugly thorns."

The thorn bush was not unhappy at these unkind words, but oftentimes it was lonely. God took pity on the thorn bush just as He pitied the poor Hebrew slaves in Egypt.

One night the thorn bush was aflame. It burned and burned, yet it did not burn up. All its branches were the brilliant red of fire. The glow of the burning bush cast a light out into the wilderness. It lighted the path of a lonely shepherd who had lost his way.

As the shepherd came toward the bush, the voice of God cried, "Moses, Moses, do not come too close. Take off your shoes, for you are on holy ground."

Moses took off his shoes. He crouched to the ground and hid his face, for he was afraid.

The voice of God spoke again, "I am the God of your fathers—Abraham, Isaac, and Jacob. I have seen how My people have suffered in Egypt. The time has come when I will take them out of Egypt into a land of milk and honey, the land of Canaan. Come, Moses, I will send you to Pharaoh, that you may bring My people out of Egypt."

Moses said, "Who am I that I should go to Pharaoh and bring the children of Israel out of Egypt?"

God said, "I shall be with you and guide you."

"But when I come to the people and say, 'the God of your fathers has sent me,' they will ask His name. What shall I tell them?"

God said, "I am that I am—tell them the Lord has sent you."

He crouched to the ground and hid his face.

"They will not listen to me," said Moses. "I will have no sign to show that God has appeared to me."

"What is in your hand?"

"A rod," answered Moses.

"Throw it on the ground."

Moses threw the rod upon the ground. It became a serpent.

"Take it by the tail."

Moses took the serpent by the tail and it became a rod.

But Moses did not have enough courage for such a mighty task.

"O God," he prayed. "I cannot speak. I have not the words to move these people."

"Your brother, Aaron, will speak to them for you. You will do the deeds; he will speak for you."

Suddenly the flame disappeared. Moses was alone in the night. His fear had left him.

"The time has come for me to go back!" he cried. "O wilderness, you have given me shelter, love. and peace. God, give me the courage I need."

Moses Goes Back to Egypt

AARON, Moses' brother, stood alone at a pass of a mountain. He could see two worlds. To the west, lay the sea, and beyond that Egypt. To him, the fertile fields and beautiful temples of Egypt meant suffering and slavery. But the east was a land of hope. Here lay the land God had promised Israel centuries before. Here he could be free and happy.

Aaron kept watching the rugged trail that led down the other side of the mountain. Would he really see his brother, Moses, again? Or was it only a dream in which he had heard the voice of God telling him to meet Moses in this place?

As though suddenly placed before him, Aaron saw an old man leading a train of donkeys up the trail. He was tall and powerful. His hair and beard were long and white, while in his hand was a staff.

As Aaron looked at the sunburnt face of the man

he stepped back and rubbed his eyes. He recognized his brother, Moses.

"Moses!" he cried, and ran up to him and kissed him.

"Aaron, my brother!" There were tears in his eyes. Forty years had passed since the brothers had seen each other.

Then Moses told Aaron of the burning bush, and how God had given him signs with which to over-awe the Egyptians. When he had finished, he said, "Is it true that all the people who knew me are dead? That it is safe for me to return to Egypt?"

"They are all dead, but the new Pharaoh is more cruel than his father. You need fear no one, Moses."

Moses went on into Egypt with Aaron. The elders of all the tribes came out to meet them.

Aaron spoke to them saying, "God has spoken to my brother, Moses, through a bush which burned and yet was not burned up. Our days of suffering are over, for across the sea is a land of milk and honey, a land where we will be free men, where we will be masters instead of slaves. Behold the signs of God!"

Moses threw his staff down. It became a serpent.

He grasped it by the tail and it became a staff.

Aaron cried, "Do you believe?"

The people cried, "We believe!"

"Will you follow our leader, Moses?"

"We will follow our leader, Moses!"

Then all the people bowed their heads and worshiped God.

Moses and Aaron Talk to Pharaoh

MOSES and Aaron came to the Pharaoh's palace. As they stood beside the tall pillars of the hall, Moses thought they looked like the oak trees of the wilderness. Men had built the great pillars of stone: poor slaves like the Hebrews had built them. Beside them, the Pharaoh looked like a fly. Moses felt greater courage than ever before in his life. He quickly walked down the aisle between the pillars to the Pharaoh's throne which was at the end of the hall.

The new Pharaoh was much like his father. His face was hard and cruel. All the wealth of the world seemed his, for the throne was made of precious stones, and his clothing was made of gold. At either side stood the priests and magicians of Egypt. They were old men with long beards and ugly faces.

Moses and Aaron bowed to the ground. Aaron

spoke, "We have heard the voice of the God of Israel and He has said, 'Let my people go into the wilderness and hold a feast to me.'"

Pharaoh said, "Who is this God that I should listen to His voice? What is His name? What has He done?"

Moses answered, "His name is God of Mercy."

Then Pharaoh turned to the priests and said, "Look in your records and see if you find the name of this God."

The priests said, "We have found the names of all other gods but not this one."

The Pharaoh laughed. "What are His deeds? Is He old or young? Has He captured cities? How long has He ruled?"

Moses said, "His power fills the universe. He was, before the world saw light. He will be, when the world is no more. He made you, great Pharaoh. With His spirit you breathe."

The Pharaoh became angry. He turned to the magicians and said, "Have you heard of this God?"

"Yes," said the chief magician. "But, great Pharaoh, what are the wonders of this God?"

It became a serpent.

122

"Show a wonder," cried the Pharaoh.

Aaron threw his rod upon the ground. It became a serpent.

The Pharaoh laughed. "This is no wonder. That is an old trick. My magicians have known it since time began."

All the magicians laughed with Pharaoh. They threw their rods on the ground and they, too, became serpents. But wonder of wonders! The serpent from Aaron's rod ate up all the magicians' serpents.

The Pharaoh was very angry and frightened. "I will not listen to this God. Israel will not leave Egypt. But they will work all the harder. Until now they were given straw for their bricks. From this hour on, they will have to gather straw for their bricks. No rest for the slaves! Let them work from sun to sun!"

Moses and Aaron fled from the palace. Moses prayed to God, saying, "Since I have spoken to the Pharaoh, he has made the people suffer even more. He will not let them go."

God said to Moses, "I will make the Pharaoh let My people go. Have courage, My servant, Moses."

"Make way for the Pharaoh,
Make way for the King,
Most holy! Most mighty!
Come, bow down, come, sing!"

THE Pharaoh stepped out of his chariot to pray
to the gods of the river Nile. He fell to the ground
while the priests chanted:

"Father Nile,
Giver of Life,
Thou makest a garden of a desert,
Thou quenchest man's thirst.
Who is greater than thee, Father Nile?"

The figure of Moses stood before them. He cried,
"The God of the Hebrews has sent me saying, 'Let
My people go, that they may serve Me in the Wilder-

ness.' You have not listened. Yet you pray to the god of the river. But the river is no god, for behold what I will do."

Aaron held his rod over the Nile. The water turned to blood. All the fish in the river died; there was a terrible odor.

The Pharaoh and all his servants ran away from the river. For seven days all the water in Egypt was turned into blood. The people came before the palace and cried, "We are thirsty. Our crops are dying. If we do not have water soon, all of us will die!"

But the Pharaoh would not listen to either the voice of God or the voice of his people. He remained stubborn and cruel.

After seven days had passed, the water became fresh. Moses and Aaron again went to the Pharaoh. They said, "Once again we ask you to let us go. If you refuse, we will bring frogs into the entire land of Egypt."

The Pharaoh cried, "Leave the palace! I will never let Israel go."

Soon there was a terrible noise. "What is that noise?" cried the Pharaoh.

Pharaoh wept—"Go out from the land of Egypt."

126

"Croak! croak! croak!
An army of frogs are we,
Into the house
Into the bed,
Into the cooking
Into the bread,
Croak! croak! croak!
An army of frogs are we."

The whole palace was filled with frogs. Grand-father frogs who croaked in a deep bass voice, and mama and papa frogs who sang in a high-pitched tenor, and tiny baby frogs who squeaked until the Pharaoh thought he would become deaf.

He called for Moses and Aaron. "Pray to your God to take these frogs away and I will let your people go."

At these words, all the frogs died and Egypt again was peaceful.

Still Pharaoh would not let Israel go. Like small imps the rest of the plagues came upon the Egyptians. As the Egyptians saw how terrible the beautiful land of Egypt had become, they again went to the Pharaoh's palace and cried, "Rid the land of the plagues! Mighty Pharaoh, let these people go!"

Pharaoh would not even listen to the voice of his people.

A terrible hail destroyed the crops. Then locusts came and ate up what was left in the fields. The people were starving. Again they cried to Pharaoh, "Let Israel go!"

Suddenly the son of the Pharaoh died. All the first born in Egypt were touched by the Angel of Death.

The Pharaoh wept, for he had lost the child he loved the most. He called Moses and Aaron and said, "Take all your flocks, all your people, and go out from the land of Egypt."

The people of Egypt all gathered around the palace and cried, "Go, Israel; go quickly!"

The Hebrews Celebrate Passover

MOSES and Aaron sent messengers who ran from house to house of the Hebrews, crying, "Pack up everything that belongs to you. We will leave the land of Egypt forever."

The people packed their clothing and household goods in huge bundles and tied them to the cattle. They gathered up all the food they could find. The time was so short they did not have time to bake any bread, so they took plain dough. Within a few hours, all the children of Israel were marching toward the wilderness.

Moses and Aaron led the army of Hebrews. Men, women, and children followed behind them. There were even some Egyptians among them, who hoped for freedom in the promised land. That night when they made camp, Moses spoke to the people, "Take the dough and spread it out so that the sun will bake it. Always remember this day, the day when you came out of Egypt, out of slavery. We shall celebrate this day every year for seven days. We will eat unleavened bread and make a feast to God."

So all the children of Israel celebrated the first Passover. That was three thousand years ago. When spring comes, we still celebrate the Passover. Today we eat matzos just as the children of Israel ate the unleavened bread which was baked in the sun. Let us pretend that one of Moses' little sons came to a Passover feast at the home of two modern children called Joseph and Rachel.

Gershom was sunburned and dark. He wore a girdle of sheepskin, for he lived in a warm country and did not need much clothing. He had come into the modern Jewish home of Joseph and Rachel, a boy and girl about his own age. How he got there was very simple. He lived in the big book which contained the Seder Service. And he came to life because we are pretending he did.

The table was set for Passover. Gershom had never before seen such a snowy white cloth. He was dazzled by the shining plates and glasses. He picked up a silver fork to see what it was like. It looked like a little silver hand. He had never seen such a beautiful table before.

Suddenly a voice cried, "Who are YOU?"

Gershom turned around to see Joseph and Rachel. He answered, "My name is Gershom."

"Where did you come from?"

"Out of that big book." He pointed to a big thick book beside grandfather's plate.

Rachel was delighted. "You mean you are one of the children of Israel?"

"Yes, I am the son of Israel's great leader, Moses. Things have changed since the first Passover. But I can tell you why each of these dishes of food is put on the table. I have lived in that book so long that I know it by heart."

"We have never been to a Passover service before, for we are only six years old," said Joseph, who was greatly interested. "What is covered up by grandfather's plate?"

Gershom answered, "Those are the matzos or unleavened bread. It is the bread we ate when we were slaves of the Egyptians."

Gershom took the hands of the children.

132

Then Joseph asked, "Why is that half burned bone placed on the table?"

Gershom replied, "Just before the children of Israel left Egypt, Moses said, 'Roast a lamb as a sacrifice to God.' The lamb was a holy animal to the Egyptians, but the Hebrews held the Lord higher than all the gods of the Egyptians."

"Why is this green horse-radish put here?" asked Rachel, picking up a sprig.

Gershom made a face. "Horse-radish is bitter. In Egypt, we suffered bitterly. We had to build great store cities, while the Egyptians beat us and gave us no rest."

"Isn't Passover a happy holiday?" asked Joseph. "Why do we have wine and good food?"

"It is a very happy holiday," Gershom smiled. "We drink wine and eat parsley or other vegetables. Spring is here. The trees become green and the flowers blossom. It is a happy time."

"What do you do after the feast?" Rachel questioned.

"We dance and sing songs. Let us join hands and I will teach you a Passover song." Gershom took the

hands of the two children and began to dance and
sing this song:

> "A kid, a kid,
> My father bought a kid,
> With two pieces of money.
> My father bought a kid."

The children laughed merrily. They suddenly
heard voices in another room.

"Who are those people?" asked Gershom.

"They are our parents and grandparents ready to
celebrate Passover."

"Then I must be going. Remember all the things
I have told you. As long as you understand the story
of Passover, you will enjoy it. Good night."

And before Rachel and Joseph could answer,
Gershom walked right back into the book of the
Seder Service and was gone.

They Cross the Red Sea

PHARAOH sat upon his throne surrounded by all the priests and magicians. A soldier bowed low before him. "O mighty one, the Hebrews have gone. They have taken everything, all their cattle, all their household goods and even some Egyptians have gone with them."

"Dogs!" cried Pharaoh. "So they left in the night. Which way did they go?"

"Toward the Red Sea."

"Isn't that the longest way? The fools will never be able to cross the sea; they have no boats."

"Their God is with them, O Pharaoh. By day He leads them with a pillar of cloud. By night He lights the way with a pillar of fire!"

"Why does this God lead them into the sea instead of by land?"

"The people to the north are very warlike. This

135

God wants to protect them from war. There are many women and children."

"What do you say, O wise men of Egypt? Shall we allow these people who have killed our children and ruined our land of Egypt to go unharmed?"

"Let us follow them," said the wise men of Egypt. "Let us take six hundred chariots and our finest soldiers. We will soon overtake them."

The next day, Pharaoh rode out into the wilderness at the head of the six hundred horsemen. What a colorful sight it was! Their brilliant head-dresses flashed in the sunlight.

Soon they came upon the band of Hebrews at the Red Sea. When the children of Israel saw the Egyptians, they were afraid. They cried to Moses, "Have you taken us out of Egypt to die in the wilderness? Look, the Pharaoh and all his men are upon us."

"Do not be afraid at the sight of the Egyptians. The Lord will take care of you."

The voice of God said, "Moses, wave your rod over the sea and divide it. Then you and the children of Israel will cross over on dry land."

Moses waved his rod and the Red Sea divided in two. The Hebrews crossed to the other side safely.

When the Pharaoh saw that the Hebrews had crossed the sea safely, he cried, "Into the sea, all of you! Let not a single Hebrew live!"

But the Pharaoh spoke too late. For no sooner had the Egyptians driven into the sea than the waters closed together upon them and they were drowned.

When the Hebrews found themselves safe on the opposite bank, they thanked God with prayer and song. The girls danced and sang.

Miriam, Moses' sister, sang this song:

"The Lord is my strength and my song,
And He is become my salvation.
He is my God and I will glorify Him.
My father's God and I will exalt Him."

The Amalekites Fight the Hebrews

Out of the wilderness they came. The air was gray with dust and the sound of their battle cry, "Ai! Ai! Ai!" echoed for miles around.

"The desert men! The desert men! To the hills with the women and children! Joshua will lead the men to fight."

Joshua and all the men went out to meet the desert men. The Amalekites were frightened by the shining swords and the numbers of the Hebrews. Joshua was able to drive them back in time to save the women and children and animals.

Joshua was the leader, young and fearless. Moses saw that he was a born general. That is why he chose him to lead the Hebrew army.

Moses climbed to the top of the hill. Here he could see for miles and signal the fighting men below. Aaron and Hur, an old man, were with him.

138

"Each of you take my hands and hold them up."

Moses held his hands up. As long as he did this, Israel won. Joshua had driven the Amalekites far from the camp.

Moses said, "I am so tired, I must rest my hands."

As soon as he put down his hands, the Amalekites began to win. Moses said, "Look, we are losing. Come, give me a rock to sit on. Then each of you take one of my hands and hold it up."

The sun beat down upon them with a terrific heat. The sweat rolled down his face, but Moses sat still, his hands toward heaven.

The soldiers looked toward the mountain. They saw Moses, his beautiful white beard flowing in the wind, his hands raised toward heaven. On they rushed. The Amalekites had left their horses. They were fighting man to man.

Suddenly the sky became black. Rain came down like rivers. Moses did not move. Just as he had withstood the scorching sun, now he braved the thunder and lightning to keep his hands raised toward heaven. Aaron and Hur faithfully held them up. Even through the rain, the soldiers could see that Moses had not left them.

Joshua cried, "Courage, men! One last charge and the Amalekites are no more. Onward! Onward!"

With even greater courage they fought the Amalekites.

At last the rain stopped. The sun had sunk below the hills. The Amalekites were completely conquered.

Moses' arms fell to his sides. He said, "We shall be a great nation, my brother. Those men are no longer slaves; they are free men. Let us build an altar to God."

So they built an altar to God.

Life in the Wilderness

MILES and miles of dry waste with only an occasional clump of trees and bushes—that was the wilderness. In the daytime the sun cast such heat that even the animals drooped. At night the wild beasts watched the camp fires, their eyes gleaming out of the darkness.

No wonder the children of Israel began to lose hope of seeing the promised land. All the food supply was gone. Then the water was gone, for there was not a stream for miles around. The people cried, "Moses, Moses, why have you brought such suffering upon us? In Egypt we worked hard, but we, at least, had food. Here we shall die of starvation and thirst."

Moses heard the cries of his people. He could not bear to look at the women and children, for they seemed to suffer most of all. At last they came to a stream. How eagerly they rushed to drink the water! But the water was bitter. Then Moses cast a tree into the water and it became sweet. The people put their mouths into the stream and drank. They felt much better after the cooling drink.

Moses said, "Do not give up hope. If you will obey God, He will watch over us and give us food." He cried to all the people, "Do you believe in the Lord?"

They answered, "We believe!"

Suddenly the pillar of cloud, which led the way, became very bright. The voice of God could be heard speaking to Moses, "I have seen how My people are suffering from hunger. At evening you will eat meat, and in the morning you will eat bread."

The people could hardly believe such a wonder could happen. Yet that evening, just as the sun sank behind the hills, a great flock of quails flew about the camp. The boys and men caught the birds, and the women cooked the meat.

The next morning when they awoke, the entire camp was white with dew. The people ran out crying, "Manna! What is it?" They put it into their mouths. It was bread and they were satisfied.

Moses picked up the white stuff and said, "It is bread; God has sent it. Remember, only gather enough bread for one day." There were some people in the camp who were greedy, and when the bread or manna rained from heaven, they gathered more than their share. But it did not do them any good. When they would try to eat the manna the next day it was sour.

"On the sixth day," Moses said to the people, "gather enough for two days, for the seventh day is the Sabbath."

After that the people worshiped God on the Sabbath.

The Commandments Are Given

THE mountains stood out against the sky, tall and pointed. Mount Sinai, the closest, was the most rugged. Yet the valley at its feet was green and fertile.

Moses said, "We will make our camp here." The children of Israel made camp at the foot of Mount Sinai.

That night, when all the camp fires were lighted, Moses called all the leaders of the tribes together and said, "I have heard the voice of God calling me to the mountain top. Take care of my people while I am gone."

Moses, staff in hand, began to climb the mountain. Overhead the sky was black and storm clouds were gathering. The path was very steep and sharp rocks cut his feet. He held his cloak about him, for a cold wind was blowing from the north.

When he reached the mountain top, the wind was so strong it almost carried him away. But Moses was unafraid, for he felt that God was near.

Crash! The heavens opened up with a flash of lightning as bright as day! The rain came down, black and heavy, soaking every rock and crevice of the mountain. Moses cringed under a large over-hanging rock. His body was soaked with rain.

All fear left Moses. His face was as bright as an Angel's. He waited for each clap of thunder. As thunder followed lightning, Moses taught Israel the commandments of God.

Thou shalt have no other gods before me.

Remember the Sabbath day to keep it holy.

Honor thy father and thy mother.

So the Lord gave the children of Israel commandments and told them how to live happily.

The sky became as peaceful as if no storm had raged. Moses picked up the two stones into which he had hewed the Commands of God. This was God's law. He would carry the tablets of stone down the mountain to the people.

The Golden Calf

DOWN in the plain, the people sat about the camp fires and grumbled.

"What has become of our leader, Moses?" cried the women.

"Why has he left us here in the wilderness to die?" cried the men.

Aaron said, "Be patient, he will come back. God watches over him."

Then all the people cried, "We do not believe in this God. Make us a god we can see, a god like the Egyptians worshiped."

Aaron did not know what to do. The people were very angry. So he said, "Bring me all your gold and silver. Take your wives' earrings and bracelets. I will make you a god to worship."

So all the people brought their gold and silver. They threw it into the fire to melt, and sang:

"Melt, melt, gold so bright,
  Shining and yellow in the night,
  Make us a god that we can see,
  Then we'll pray and bend the knee."

When the gold was all melted. Aaron molded it into a golden calf.

"This is our god, O Israel, who brought us out of the land of Egypt. Let us make a feast to it, our god."

Early the next morning they arose. But the people did not pray to the golden calf. They danced and sang:

"O golden calf, O golden calf,
  To you we dance and sing.
  O golden calf, O golden calf,
  For you our praises ring."

Faster and faster they danced. The day wore on and night crept upon them. They did not see Moses as he came down the mountain with the two tablets in his hands. He saw them dancing. He lifted the two tablets above his head and threw them on the ground. They broke with a loud crash which rang out like

He threw the calf into the fire.

149

thunder. The people were frightened. They covered their eyes with their hands. Moses strode into the camp. He threw the calf into the fire. The flames leapt up and melted it to a lump of metal. Moses trampled it into powder and threw it into the water.

"Why have you done such a thing?" he cried to his brother, Aaron.

Aaron answered, "I could not keep them here otherwise."

Then Moses raised his hands high, and cried, "O wicked people, are there none among you who are on the side of the Lord?"

All the men of the tribe of Levi came and stood beside him.

Moses prayed to God, "The people have sinned a great sin. Wilt Thou forgive them?"

The Lord answered, "Lead My people out of this place. I will send an Angel to guide you."

So Moses led them on into the wilderness. His heart was sad at what they had done.

Then Moses heard the voice of God, saying, "Go up to Mount Sinai again. Write out the law that the people may always know it."

Moses went up to the top of Mount Sinai again. He did not eat bread or drink water. But for forty days and forty nights, he pounded out the Ten Commandments on tablets of stone.

When his work was finished, he came down the mountain. Aaron and all the children of Israel were there to meet him. As he gave them the Ten Commandments, his face was as bright as the sun.

Bezalel Builds the Tabernacle

Moses called all the children of Israel together and said, "Six days of the week you may work, but the seventh day is a holy day, a day when you worship God. We must have a fitting place to worship. We must have a place to keep the law. Come, let us build a tabernacle to God."

This pleased the people, and they said, "Yes, let us build a tabernacle to God."

Then Moses said, "We must have materials for the tabernacle. We need gold, silver, and brass. Here is a chance for every man and woman in Israel to help build the tabernacle. Remember, give because you want to give."

The people cried, "We will all build the tabernacle."

They began to bring their offerings, and soon there was so much gold, silver, and brass that Moses had to tell them to stop bringing gifts. Moses said, "If each person brings a gift, then everybody will help to build the tabernacle."

So the work on the tabernacle began. The camp was busier and happier than ever before.

A man called Bezalel was in charge of the work. He built a huge forge. Soon the red flames of the fire began to leap up and down from the forge. The cling and clang of the goldsmiths' hammers rang merrily through the camp. First the gold was melted into a shapeless lump, but under the workmen's skilled hands it became breastplates for the priests, candlesticks, and other ornaments for the tabernacle.

Another group of men went into the mountains and cut down acacia trees. They sawed the wood into poles and boards. These poles were fitted together into a framework which looked like a large tent. The poles had to fit into each other perfectly because the tabernacle had to be taken apart and moved from place to place.

One of the busiest spots in the entire camp was where the women wove the cloth which was to be used for the priests' robes and for curtains. As their spinning wheels hummed and whirled the women sang:

"We will weave a cloth so fine,
It will gleam and it will shine.
Strong as flint, yet soft as feathers,
It will stand the harshest weathers."

When the tabernacle was finished, all the people marveled at the beautiful piece of work. They thanked Bezalel, for he had showed them how to build it.

The outside of the tabernacle looked like a great big tent. It was covered with skins of animals dyed red. Inside hung linen curtains dyed blue, purple, and scarlet. The poles were joined together with brass sockets. All the ornaments were made of gold. These included a table with a solid gold top, gold vases, and candlesticks. The altar was decorated with gold and even the bowl which contained the oil for the everlasting light was made of gold.

Aaron and his sons, who were the priests, wore robes of finest linen, with belts of blue, purple, and scarlet. They wore breastplates of gold and precious stones.

When all was ready, Moses entered the tabernacle first. He put the beautiful robes on Aaron and his sons. He anointed their heads with oil. Then Moses blessed them and made them priests.

Moses next blessed all the children of Israel. All Israel rejoiced in the great work they had done.

Moses Appoints Judges

ONE day a caravan stopped by Israel's camp at the foot of Mount Sinai. Everyone was excited, and they all ran out to see the strangers. There was an old man, a young woman, and two boys. Imagine the surprise of the Israelites when they saw Moses greet the strangers affectionately. They were none other than Moses' wife, Zipporah, his two sons, Gershom and Eliezer, and his father-in-law, Jethro.

Moses was very happy to see his family again, and he took them into his tent.

Jethro said, "We have heard of all that God has done for you, even in the land of Midian. Tell us all that has happened."

Moses told them all that God had done to Pharaoh and the Egyptians for Israel's sake. He told them how they had crossed the Red Sea and of all their hardships in the wilderness.

Jethro answered, "Blessed be the Lord who has delivered you from the Egyptians. Now I know that the Lord is greater than all the gods. Come, let us offer up a burnt offering to God!"

Moses called Aaron and all the elders together, and they offered a sacrifice to God. Then they held a feast for Jethro.

The next day Jethro decided to look over the camp. The women were busy at their household tasks, and the men were tending the sheep.

Suddenly there arose a great noise. Jethro rushed over to find the cause of the trouble. Two shepherds were quarreling over a lamb. They were so angry that they almost came to blows.

"Tell your quarrels to Moses," cried the people. "He is the judge."

So the two shepherds carried the lamb to Moses' tent which was in the center of the camp. Moses sat on a throne like a king. Many people were gathered around him. Each in his turn brought his little quarrels for Moses to judge.

One of the shepherds said, "We will have to wait here all day, there are so many here before us."

"Can't you settle this yourselves?" asked Jethro. "Then you can go back to work in peace."

"That's right," said the other shepherd. "Why should we waste all day over one little lamb. You take the lamb. When it is fattened, we will kill it. Give me my half and I will be satisfied."

"That is fair enough," answered the other, and they went their way the best of friends.

Jethro looked after them. He said, "If only given a chance, these people can govern themselves."

That night he went into Moses' tent. Moses was very tired after his day of labor.

Jethro said, "You are wasting your energy trying to do everything yourself. These people can govern themselves." He told Moses the story of the two shepherds.

Moses said, "You are right, Jethro, but what should I do?"

Jethro said, "Appoint men as judges over the people. Choose only the wisest and the most just men."

Moses did as Jethro suggested. He appointed judges to help the people decide their questions.

This was a good thing for Israel. It taught the people to govern themselves and prepared them for the time when they would enter the promised land.

The Scouts Go to Palestine

〜〇〜

THE children of Israel were encamped in the wilderness of Paran. Not far away, just over the mountains, lay the promised land. But it was no easy task to enter the land of Canaan, because it was said to be inhabited by a very strong and warlike people.

Moses called a meeting of all the tribes. He said, "We need a man from each tribe to help spy out the land. It is a hard task to be a scout. A man must have great courage; he must be able to withstand hunger and thirst. He must not be afraid of death."

For a moment everyone was silent and then a young man stepped forward and said, "I will go." His name was Joshua. He was strong and tall, and his face was eager and fearless.

"I, too, will go," said another man. His name was Caleb. He was young and strong, also.

For a moment there was silence again. Then a

shout went up for Joshua and Caleb. When the other young men saw that the people admired the courage of the two volunteers, they quickly offered to go. Soon there was a scout from each tribe, and as they stood in a row before Moses, the people shouted, "Hurrah for the scouts!"

Moses said, "I am glad that all of you are going of your own free will. Get ready for a long journey and come to my tent at dawn, and I will give you directions."

The scouts were ready to leave at sunrise. Each man carried a supply of food on his back. He also carried a gourd of water. He carried a knife and bow and arrows in case of danger or to hunt for food.

Moses looked each man over carefully to see that he was well prepared for the journey. Then he said, "Go south from here and enter the land by way of the mountains. This is the information I want. First, what is the size of the country? See if the people are strong or weak, and if there are many of them. See if the land is good or bad; if there is plenty of wood and water. Let me know if the people live in camps or in well-guarded cities. Remember, be of good courage and bring back some of the fruit of the land."

So with Joshua leading the way, the scouts started on their journey.

It was a hard journey over the mountains, and the food supply soon gave out. They lived on wild game which they hunted. The men were tired and weary. Imagine their delight with their first glimpse of the promised land.

It was in the fall of the year and the grapes were just beginning to ripen. Stacks of golden grain stood in the fields, and the trees were laden with fruit.

To these homeless wanderers it seemed like a dream. "What large grape clusters!" they cried. "What huge stalks of grain!" In this manner they marveled at everything they saw.

The people of the land were tall and sunburned, and some of the scouts were afraid of them and called them giants. They were completely overawed by the cities. The cities were well guarded and the scouts feared to enter them. So they cut down the largest clusters of grapes they could find. They picked figs and pomegranates and carried them all back to Israel's camp in the wilderness.

It seemed like a dream.

163

One of the scouts said, "As you see, it is a land of milk and honey, but the people are very fierce. They are as tall as giants. They live in well-guarded cities and should we even try to take the land away from them, they would kill us all off."

"It is not so," cried Joshua. "We who live in the desert are used to hardships, and we are stronger than these people. We could conquer them very easily."

But the people believed the story of the giants and they turned to Moses and cried, "It is your fault. You, who took us away from our homes in Egypt. Now you want us to be killed by giants."

"Be quiet," commanded Moses. "Strength alone is not enough to take the land. We must have courage. O people of little courage, this land is not for you! None of you shall ever set foot on the land, but we shall wander here in the desert until all of you have died, and your children have grown to manhood. A new and fearless race shall inherit the land!"

And so the children of Israel turned their backs on the promised land and began their wanderings which were to last for forty years.

Blessings Instead of Curses

THE children of Israel roamed through many lands during the forty years they spent in the wilderness. Some of the people were warlike. They fought these people and conquered them so that all the surrounding countries were afraid of them.

There was a king named Balak. He ruled over the land of Moab. When he heard that the children of Israel were coming into his country, he was afraid. He called all the wise men and said, "These people have conquered all the countries into which they wander. Their God watches over them. No matter what we do, they will conquer us."

The wise men said, "Great King Balak, there is a prophet called Balaam. He is said to be as great as Moses. Send messengers to this prophet Balaam and see if he can help you."

King Balak did as the wise men told him. He sent

the princes of Moab as messengers to Balaam. They said, "Balak, our king, has sent us here. There is a people who have come out of Egypt. They have conquered all who are in their way. You are a great prophet, Balaam. Come with us and curse these people that they may not be able to conquer us."

Balaam answered, "Stay in my house tonight. I will give you my answer in the morning."

That night God spoke to Balaam in a dream and said, "You shall not go with the princes of Moab. You shall not curse these people, for they are blessed."

Balaam told the princes of his dream. When they returned home, Balak, the king, was angry. He said, "I will send Balaam gifts of gold and silver. Perhaps this will make him curse these people."

When Balaam saw all the gold and silver, he did not know what to do. He said, "Stay in my house for the night. In the morning I will tell you what I will do."

That night he again heard the voice of God, who said, "Go with these men, Balaam. But only speak the words I tell you to speak."

There before his eyes stood an angel with a flaming sword in his hand.

167

Early the next morning, Balaam set out with the messengers. They rode for a while. Suddenly Balaam's donkey stopped and would not move.

"Get up there!" cried Balaam in anger. The donkey moved against a wall and hurt Balaam's foot. He kicked the donkey.

This time she lay down on the ground and refused to move. Balaam was so angry he began to beat the poor donkey with his stick. The beast could stand it no longer and cried, "Why do you beat me, master Balaam? Have I ever done this to you before? I cannot go on now."

Balaam stopped beating the donkey. There, before his eyes, stood an angel with a flaming sword in his hand. The angel said, "It is true, the donkey could not go on, for I stood in her way. Remember, Balaam, go with the men, but speak only what I shall tell you to speak."

The donkey got up and began to move along as quickly as it could.

Soon Balaam came to the border of the country of Moab. Balak, himself, had come to meet the prophet. He said, "Why did you not come when I first sent for you, Balaam? Am I not worthy of honoring you?"

Balaam answered, "I can only speak the words the Lord puts into my mouth. Build seven altars and sacrifice seven sheep. Then I shall tell you the word of the Lord."

When the sacrifices were ready, Balaam spoke:

"The King of Moab from the mountains of the East,
  Has brought a poor prophet to pray and to feast,
  How shall I curse whom God has not cursed?
  These people whom God has blessed from the
    first."

Balak was angry. He cried, "I brought you here to curse these people—not to bless them."

Balaam answered, "I can only say what the Lord tells me to say."

Balak thought that if he took the prophet to another part of the country, he would speak differently. Again seven altars were built. Again seven sheep were sacrificed.

When Balak said to the prophet, "Speak, O Balaam," he answered:

"Arise, O Balak, and hear, give ear,
The Lord hath spoken, His word I keep,
And when He hath blessed I cannot call it back.
Israel shall become a mighty nation.
This beautiful land shall be His."

When Balak heard these words, he was very angry. Yet he could do nothing with the prophet. So he said, "Go your way, Balaam, and I will go mine."

So the children of Israel were saved from the cruel king, Balak, and entered the country of Moab in peace.

The Waters of Meribah

ISRAEL wandered in the wilderness for forty years. During that time all the old people died. Their children grew up to be strong and brave. But Moses, Aaron, and Miriam had grown old. Miriam could not stand the hardships of the desert and she, too, died. When she was gone, all the water dried up. There was not a drop of rain for months. The people were dying of thirst. They came to Moses' tent and cried, "Moses, give us water, or we shall all die."

Moses was very unhappy over the death of his sister. In his grief, he lost patience with these people he had watched over so long. He fell upon his face and prayed to God, saying, "O God, give us water that all your people may not die of thirst."

God said, "Take the rod I have given you. Lead the people to a rock I will show you. Speak to the rock and it will give you water."

When all the people were gathered at the rock, they were impatient. They cried, "Where is your water, Moses? Show us your water."

Moses was angry. He struck the rock with all his might. Crash! The water flowed forth like a torrent. The people rushed into the water like madmen, so eager were they to drink. Even the cattle rushed to cool their parched throats.

But God was angry with Moses and Aaron. God said, "I told you to speak to the rock, not to strike it. I have forgiven these people all during the years of hardship. I warned you to be kind to them. In anger, you disobeyed my words. Therefore, neither of you shall enter the promised land."

When Moses heard these words, he was very sad. He knew that his time on earth was drawing to a close. He knew that Israel must have a leader. So he called Joshua, who was not only a good man but a leader of men as well.

"Behold, Joshua, I give these people into your hands. They are a young nation. Have patience with them. Be a stern leader. Do not allow them to fall into wicked ways."

Crash! The water flowed forth like a torrent.

173

Joshua answered, "O my teacher, Moses, I am not worthy of so high an office."

But Moses said, "Come here that I may kiss you."

Joshua knelt. Moses kissing him, said, "May you be at peace and may Israel be at peace with you."

The Hebrews Overcome the Amorites

ISRAEL left the mountains behind them. They were now encamped in the fertile plains of the Amorites. The Amorites were warlike and very unfriendly. Their king was called Sihon. He was very cruel.

One night Joshua came into Moses' tent, crying, "Sihon, king of the Amorites, is marching toward us with thousands of men. What should we do? Defend the camp or go out to meet them?"

"We will go out to meet them!" answered Moses.

Soon every man was ready for the fight. Each man was armed with a sword and a torch.

The glare of the torches lighted up the plain. As one man they sang this song:

"Sihon, King of the Amorites, beware,
We come to fight with sword and flare;

Your cities, your palaces are no more
The host of Israel has gone before."

When Sihon saw the Hebrews approaching, he was afraid. After very little fighting his whole army fled before the Hebrews.

By morning, Heshbon, capital city of the Amorites, was in the hands of the Hebrews. Moses made his headquarters in Heshbon. From this point he sent out spies. They went into the surrounding countries and reported their strength to Moses.

The spies said, "All the surrounding countries bow to us, Moses. But there is one king called Og. He is the most terrible of them all. He is a giant. Everyone fears him."

Moses said, "Let our men rest for a while. We must be ready to meet this giant, and tired men are poor fighters."

So the children of Israel stayed in Heshbon for a long time.

The Story of Giant Og

Og, KING of Bashan, was the last king for the Israelites to conquer before they entered the promised land. It is true that he ruled over sixty cities which were surrounded by high walls, in which were gates with bars, but there was no reason to fear him. In spite of his tremendous size, Og was weak. He had gained his power through the silly stories which had grown up about him.

When people spoke of Og, they did not talk about an ordinary man. They described him as a giant who ate a thousand lambs in one day. They said that he was five hundred years old—that he was as tall as an oak tree and as strong as a rock.

But the most interesting thing about Og was his bedstead. It was supposed to have been made of iron, a very rare thing in those days; and it was said to have been eight feet wide and eighteen feet long.

It was not strange that the children of Israel should have been afraid of this giant. Some of them came to Moses and said:

"Perhaps we cannot conquer Og. According to the stories people tell us, he will crush us with a single blow."

Moses answered, "Those are silly stories indeed. This man, Og, is an ordinary man. He, too, has grown to believe all the stories about himself and instead of fighting he has been content to sit in his palace and believe himself a strong man. Forget all these stories. It will be easy to conquer Og."

But a messenger came in and cried, "Og, King of Bashan, is gathering together a mighty army. He intends to revenge the death of his friend Sihon, King of the Amorites."

When Moses heard this news, he gave the command for Israel to prepare for battle again, and they marched against Og and all his followers.

When the children of Israel saw Og, they laughed at all their fears. The big, fat king of Bashan was the one who was afraid, and he turned and ran away from the Israelites.

He turned and ran away from the Israelites.

179

Og and all his followers were soon conquered, and Israel took every one of the sixty cities.

The last of the enemies of Israel was defeated, and the way was clear to enter the promised land.

The Two and a Half Tribes Help

THE River Jordan! How still and silvery the water! How green and fertile the land through which it flows! When the children of Israel saw the land, they cried, "This is the place for cattle."

There were two and a half tribes that had more cattle than all the rest. They said to Moses, "This is a land of green pastures. Since we have more cattle than all the other tribes, can't we stay on this side of the Jordan and make our homes here?"

Moses answered, "How can you stay on this side of the Jordan, when all the other tribes must fight for the land on the other side? Are you afraid of the promised land? Remember, your fathers died in the desert because they listened to the stories of the spies. They were afraid to fight for the land."

"We are not afraid," cried the shepherds. "We will fight together with our brothers until every man has settled in the promised land. All that we ask is that we may leave our wives, our children, and our cattle in this place while we go on to war."

Moses said, "Then, before I die, I will tell Joshua that the land of Gilead belongs to you and your children."

The shepherds kept their word. They crossed the Jordan and helped their brothers conquer the land. Then they returned.

When they came back, they not only settled in the land of Gilead, but they also built many beautiful cities and villages.

Moses Decides

AS THE time drew near for Israel to enter the promised land, the question of how to divide the land became very important. To avoid all question of unfairness, Moses decided to have the people draw lots for the land.

All the people gathered together and the head of each family drew his lot. When all the men had drawn their lots, one lot still remained. The man in charge cried, "There is still land left. Who has not drawn his lot?"

Everyone looked around to find the owner. Imagine their surprise to see five young girls step forward.

The man said, "This is not the place for women. This land is for men."

Then the oldest girl said, "The land belongs to our father, Zelophehad, but he died in the wilder-

"Take the land. It is yours."

184

ness. He was a good and pious man. Should he lose his inheritance because he has no sons? Give us the land; we will take care of it."

The people murmured among themselves, "What can women do with land?"

But Moses thought differently, and turning to the daughters of Zelophehad, he said, "Take the land. It is yours. If a man dies as did your father and leaves no son, then all his possessions rightfully belong to his daughters."

The daughters were so happy at this just decision of Moses that they wept with joy.

Moses looked upon the girls kindly and said, "And now that you have your land, tell me what will you do?"

They replied, "We shall marry and take good care of the land."

So the daughters of Zelophehad married the men of their choice and lived good and happy lives.

Moses Passes Away

IT WAS evening; the day's work was done. Moses stood by the door of his tent and looked over the camp of Israel. The older people sat around the camp fires and talked, while the young boys and girls sang and danced in the firelight. As Moses looked at his people, he felt a glow of happiness. How strong and fearless they were! How confident of the land just across the River Jordan!

Moses called to Joshua and Eleazar and said, "To-day I am a hundred and twenty years old; I cannot go in and come out as I used to. I am getting old."

Joshua and Eleazar said nothing. To them Moses seemed as strong and able as ever. Only his eyes looked a little tired.

Moses went on, "The Lord has told me I cannot go over the River Jordan, but that all my people shall go into the promised land. He will not forsake you."

Joshua and Eleazar were sad. Moses looked into their eyes and said, "Go now. Tell all the priests and people to gather before my tent in the morning."

So the two men left Moses alone and went to bring his message to the people.

When they had gone, Moses heard the voice of God, saying, "Behold, you are about to sleep with your fathers. These people will forget all that you have taught them. They will break the law and worship false gods. Write down your words, Moses, for the children of Israel."

When Moses heard these words, he thought of a beautiful poem, and went inside his tent to write it down.

The next morning all the priests and people were gathered outside his tent.

Moses chose Joshua to be the leader in his place, and he said to him, "Be strong and of good courage; for you shall bring the children of Israel into the promised land."

Then Moses called the priests, and they came and stood before him. He gave them a book in which he had written all the laws and said, "Take this book of the law, and put it by the ark of the covenant."

Then he sang the poem which he had written. In the song, Moses told the people of the greatness of the Lord; of His justice, and of His kindness. He told them not to forget the days of their ancestors, not to worship false gods, not to break the laws.

Moses blessed the people, saying:

"Happy art thou, O Israel, who is like unto thee?
  A people saved by the Lord.
  Thine enemies shall dwindle away before thee;
  And thou shall tread upon their high places."

Then all the people went away and left Moses alone, for that was his wish. He climbed to the top of Mount Nebo. From there he could look down and see the promised land. He filled his eyes with the sight of the green valleys, the flowing rivers, and even the distant sea. And Moses was content.

So Moses died somewhere in the land of Moab, and no man has ever seen his grave.

He died in the full vigor of manhood, and Israel has never known another leader like him.

He filled his eyes with the sight.

189